The Homebuyer's Survival Guide

Kenneth W. Edwards

Real Estate
Education Company
a division of Dearborn Financial Publishing, Inc.

While a great deal of care has been taken to provide accurate and current information, the ideas, suggestions, general principles and conclusions presented in this text are subject to local, state and federal laws and regulations, court cases and any revisions of same. The reader is thus urged to consult legal counsel regarding any points of law—this publication should not be used as a substitute for competent legal advice.

Publisher: Kathleen A. Welton
Acquisitions Editor: Patrick J. Hogan
Associate Editor: Karen A. Christensen
Senior Project Editor: Jack L. Kiburz
Editorial Assistant: Kristen G. Landreth
Interior Design: Lucy Jenkins
Cover Design: Salvatore Concialdi

Published by Real Estate Education Company,
a division of Dearborn Financial Publishing, Inc.

Printed in the United States of America

94 95 96 10 9 8 7 6 5 4 3 2

Library of Congress Cataloging-in-Publication Data

Edwards, Kenneth W., 1928–
  The homebuyer's survival guide / by Kenneth W. Edwards.
    p. cm.
  Includes bibliographical references and index.
  ISBN 0-7931-0906-X
  1. House buying.   I. Title.
  HD1379.E34 1994   94-7178
  643'.12—dc20   CIP

• •

Dedication

To Edythe Utendorffer
Journalism Teacher Emeritus
Turlock Union High School, Turlock, California

Contents

▼

Preface

·····▼·····

Let's imagine for the moment that you have the formidable task of crossing a minefield. Clearly visible on the other side is a forested path leading to an incredibly quaint little cottage, complete with white picket fence, babbling brook and smoke curling from the brick chimney. On the front door is a deed to the home with your name on it—along with a mortgage, of course. Your challenge is to get there alive and in one piece and claim your dream.

One course of action would be to head boldly and bravely across the field, trusting in your good fortune and perhaps a little divine guidance. It is entirely possible that you could complete your journey with life and limb in tact. Others have. Another option would be to secure a map of the field showing you where the mines are located, hire a trained, experienced guide who has crossed the field many times before to lead you, say a little prayer and head on out. The journey will still not be without danger, but faced with those alternatives the rational choice is clear.

While buying a home is certainly not as hazardous as tiptoeing through a minefield, there are, in fact, a number of perils a homebuyer does face, not all of which are obvious. One important example is the subject of agency, or who represents whom in a real estate transaction. Most buyers think the agent with whom they work represents them—not true in the vast majority of cases. As we will see, that's not a problem as long as you know the ground rules and act accordingly. Then there are natural perils, such as earthquakes, floods, tornadoes, sinkholes and wildfires, all of which will impact on your decision as to where to buy and how to protect your investment. Throw in civil unrest and it's a sobering prospect. Add environmental concerns such as radon, asbestos and lead paint and it gets downright scary.

My goal is to provide you a map of the minefield, act as your mentor in absentia and provide recommendations on how to secure loyal and informed professional guides to accompany you on your journey. I will discuss the homebuying process in the general order in which you will need the information, starting with establishing your specific goals, developing a strategy and doing your initial investigation. At each step I will identify several "red flags"—warning signs that could indicate your survival is about to be threatened. To counter each, I'll also offer my strategies for survival.

Buyer Beware!

If you've never purchased a home, you've got a particularly worthy challenge and it's going to take some serious study, since you are going to be crossing completely unfamiliar terrain. But don't assume that just because you've bought and sold a few homes in the past that you know as much as necessary to be an informed homebuyer. Things have changed dramatically in the past few years in the real estate profession. In financing alone, for example, the array of options a homebuyer is faced with now can be truly bewildering. Or you may have been just plain lucky on your previous home purchases to have escaped major problems. I know I certainly was.

Whether you are a single, a "mingle" (unrelated persons buying together), a "dink" (double income, no kids), an empty nester or the Ozzie and Harriet prototype family, the opportunities and challenges you will face are much the same. There may be differences in some of the details, but your basic goal—that of striving to become a satisfied homeowner—is identical.

In legal terminology there is a phrase known as "caveat emptor"— buyer beware. That's extremely good advice for homebuyers. It simply means you had better know what you're doing, inspect the goods very thoroughly and look out for your own interests at every step. No matter how much disclosure takes place, no matter who says what to whom, no matter how good and honorable (or dishonorable) the intentions, after the smoke has cleared and the money and deeds have changed hands, it is the buyer who is left to live with, and in, the end product of the whole process. The seller may be long gone to distant places. The real estate broker is busy putting together other transactions. While there have been some welcome consumer and legal developments in recent years that favor homebuyers, there are still very good reasons to be very, very wary.

Mandatory Disclosure

In the interest of full and informed disclosure, I will share some of my background and biases with you. After a career in the U.S. Air Force, in which my family and I rented, bought and sold several homes in various parts of this country and overseas, I sold real estate successfully on a full-time basis for several years in a small university town in the Pacific Northwest. Although I am still a licensed real estate agent and a REALTOR®, I now concentrate my activities on writing, speaking, consulting and teaching.

Now for my biases. I am thoroughly convinced that for most people, buying a home is an extremely wise course of action. Done properly, it can turn out to be an incredibly good monetary investment, and in most circumstances the lifestyle of the homeowner is superior to the lifestyle of the renter. If you are raising a family, the social benefits are likely to be even more pronounced. The fact that we will spend so much time identifying hazards and perils shouldn't obscure the fact that, in my opinion, owning your own home is clearly one of life's most worthwhile goals.

I also believe that, as a rule, a homebuyer's best interests will be served by working with a well-qualified, carefully chosen, licensed real estate professional. Since I identify some manipulative sales techniques that are sometimes used by real estate people and describe in some detail the identity crises the industry is presently experiencing, I do not want to give the impression that you are likely to be better off avoiding them altogether. Again, I'll give detailed guidance on choosing an agent and working with one, but you do need to know my views up front.

I suppose I should also disclose one other matter. After I return from meeting with my real estate licensing class for the first time, my wife always asks me this question: "Did you warn them about your weird sense of humor?" While not necessarily agreeing with her basic premise, I do believe that in both teaching and writing, the learning process is greatly enhanced if eyeballs are not disappearing. I am also convinced that things don't have to be dull to be credible. For those reasons I've included a few war stories and personal experiences to illustrate certain points and liven things up.

Adjust Your Sights

There are some areas of the country where a hundred thousand dollars will buy a lot of house. There are others where it may buy a lot—period. So when I discuss home prices and mortgage loans, simply adjust everything to the situation where you plan to buy your home. I should also point out that there is essentially no such thing now as a national real estate market. Even when things were disastrous in the Southwest, for example, some other areas were quite strong. About the only thing that is determined at the national level is the cost of money, or what kind of interest you will have to pay to get a mortgage loan. So if you hear some national commentator pontificating about how terrible or how terrific the real estate market is, just filter the information through your local lenses.

If you've moved around the country much, you have already discovered that while buying a house in New York State is similar to buying one in California, there are some differences. For example, in some places attorneys typically handle the closing process, while in others escrow companies, title companies, lending institutions or even real estate brokers do the closing. While procedures may differ, the process is basically the same and the desired outcome for you, the homebuyer, is identical. We will concentrate on strategies intended to help you achieve that goal.

The Language of Real Estate

Real estate does have a language all its own, and it can be intimidating to the outsider. Surveys consistently show that those who aren't in the profession find the terms confusing and a barrier to understanding. For that reason, where it is necessary I will define basic concepts in terms that are as easily understood and nontechnical as possible. I've had some experience doing that. For a couple of years I served as a consultant to our state real estate agency in producing the official real estate manual used by real estate licensees. My job was to translate what staff attorneys and other agency officials had written into what was reasonably comprehensible to we mere mortals.

Homebuying Facts of Life

If we had titled this book *How To Buy a Home in 48 Hours with No Money, No Work, No Risk and No Brains!*, perhaps we would have attracted more attention. The fact of the matter is, however, that you will need some money, it will involve work to do it right, there is a degree of risk, it will take a little time and although you certainly don't need to be intellectually gifted, it will help if you use a commonsense approach. I don't want to discourage you, however, and I obviously want you to read this book, so I will cover all the exotic possibilities such as no money down, equity sharing, foreclosures, lease options and land sales contracts. These are all legitimate topics that deserve attention, but I do want to make it clear that I subscribe strongly to what I'm told is an ancient Russian proverb: "The only free cheese is in the mousetrap!"

Okay, so it's not likely to be easy. But just keep visualizing that incredibly charming little cottage in the glen (or that castle on the hill, depending upon your circumstances) with the deed on the door with your name on it. There are few endeavors more worthy of your efforts. Our journey is about to begin. Have a safe and happy trip!

1

•••••▼•••••

Your Home Quest: The Journey Begins

Over 60 percent of all Americans own their own homes, the highest percentage in the world. It has been significantly higher than that in the past and would surely be now except for the simple fact that lately it has been tougher to afford a home. The heart of the American Dream for most of us has been and continues to be owning our own home—being the kings and queens of our own castles, no matter how modest.

Home Ownership: The Pros

My guess is that if you were not already reasonably well convinced that home ownership is a worthwhile goal, you would not be reading this book. But in the unlikely event you may have some lingering, unresolved doubts, let's at least summarize some of the major arguments for and against—the pros and cons. We will then get into the specific details.

Lifestyles of the Content and Prosperous

While there are some excellent economic reasons to own a home, the primary decision should be—I am convinced—a lifestyle choice. Singer Sophie Tucker is alleged to have uttered the immortal words: "I've been rich and I've been poor. I'll take rich." My version is: "I've been a renter and I've been a homeowner. I'll take owner." That pretty much says it for those who have been both. Here's an illustration.

• •

Trick or Treat

When I was assigned by the air force to an ROTC tour of duty at the University of California, Berkeley, we bought a new home in a moderately priced subdivision in Walnut Creek, California, a community in the San Francisco East Bay area. It was 100 percent owner-occupied single-family homes. The schools were within easy walking distance; the neighborhood was pleasant, clean and quiet; there were plenty of reasonably well-behaved playmates for our children; and we thoroughly enjoyed landscaping the yard and decorating the inside of the house. When our youngsters went around the block on Halloween, they came back happy and safe with a bag overflowing with unpoisoned candy.

While we were waiting for our new home to be finished, we rented an apartment in Walnut Creek. Even with the swimming pool in the complex and the around-the-clock laundry facilities, the quality of life could not compare to being in our own home. It was crowded and noisy and populated with at least a few residents who were definitely not "citizen of the year" candidates. Getting your car in and out of your allotted parking spot took particular skill and courage. Sirens for various emergencies were a frequent occurrence.

Would things have been more tranquil and serene if we had rented a single-family home in a bit more upscale neighborhood? Possibly, but still not even in the same ballpark. Fair it may not be. True it is. That's the reason that survey after survey shows that most renters desperately want to become homeowners and are working hard toward reaching that goal.

• •

The Road to Riches?

Is it cheaper to rent or to buy? It all depends on how you do your calculations and what assumptions you make. The out-of-pocket monthly expenses are almost always more for the homeowner. And—this may surprise you—some studies show that in many cases, even after all appropriate income tax benefits are calculated, it costs slightly less to rent than to own.

Of course, this ignores several very important factors. First, you are more likely to be happier (and safer) in a place you own rather than in one you rent. Second, if you own your home, as it appreciates in value (as homes traditionally have) the profit is yours when you sell. In the best of all scenarios your home appreciates a little (or a lot) each month, while at the same time your monthly payments reduce the principal and you owe less.

It is true that during the early years of a loan most of the monthly payment goes toward interest, but each month some does go toward reducing principal, and that amount increases monthly. Furthermore, this is absolutely the best type of savings plan—it's forced! Every time you make your mortgage payment, you are depositing money in your account. If appreciation is factored into the equation, assuming even modest growth, owning typically emerges as the better financial decision—often by an astounding degree. And if you do realize a profit, there are provisions whereby you may either defer paying taxes on the gain or have it forgiven altogether. We will cover those pleasant options in more detail later.

When you move out of a rented home or an apartment, on the other hand, the increase in value that occurred while you were a tenant goes to the landlord. If you are looking for an investment to serve as a hedge against inflation, real estate has historically been one of the best. Remember the house where we lived in Walnut Creek? We bought it in 1966 for $30,000 and sold it in 1970 for $43,500. I get faint when I think what it's worth today—over a quarter of a million!

Third, as rents go up, the total monthly principal and interest payment on your mortgage stays the same, assuming you have a fixed-rate mortgage. The folks who bought the Walnut Creek house and assumed my 30-year, 6 percent fixed-rate GI loan are still paying just over $200 per month, principal and interest. Rents in that area now, on the other hand, are in another galaxy.

Home Ownership: The Cons

While there is a lot to be said for owning your own home, there are also a few things that can be said against it.

Homes Require TLC

I once had a neighbor where we now live who was a dedicated jogger. Each afternoon he jogged down our very steep hill and walked back up. Quite often I would be mowing a large section of our side yard as he passed. Although he never said as much, I am convinced he thought I was mentally deficient for mowing the field (with a self-propelled power mower—and I was the self that provided the power), as opposed to letting it grow naturally. The fact is, as weird as it may sound, I enjoy mowing. I personally thought he was the one who needed counseling, since he started and finished at the same point each day and had nothing to show for it at the end.

Here's the point. Homes do take care, which involves an expenditure of effort and money. There is no landlord or super to call to fix the leaky toilet, and if you have to replace something major such as a hot water heater or, heaven forbid, a furnace, your budget will take a major hit. If you and your mate, if you have one, are not the types who are willing to do (or hire out) the minimum work necessary to keep the homestead looking good (inside and out) and if you resent shelling out several grand to replace the roof over your head, then perhaps renting is the better choice.

The Boom-Bust Scenario

If you buy a home for $100,000 with a 10 percent down payment and the price appreciates 10 percent in two years, you've got a paper profit of roughly $10,000, or a 100 percent return on your investment (your down payment) in two years. Not too shabby, and not at all unrealistic in certain places and certain times. However, the operative phrase is "paper profit." In reality, rapid appreciation will likely cost you money out of pocket, since your appraised value will increase as will property taxes and your casualty insurance premiums. But the point is that unless you have to sell, it makes little difference, except for taxes and insurance, how the value of your home skyrockets.

The same logic applies if the real estate market heads south and the home you bought for $100,000 is suddenly worth only $80,000 on the open market. The glitch is that if you have to sell when prices are depressed, you will lose big money. That has to be acknowledged as a risk of home ownership.

No one can predict what will happen in the future—and certainly not economists—but the past has always been the best indicator of the future. For decades home ownership in America has been a blue chip, gilt-edged, money-making investment. Do it right and hang on to it long enough, and there's a strong likelihood that it will be a good investment for you. So if it's the lifestyle you think you prefer, you may well end up getting a lot richer while you live that good life.

Build It and They Will Come (and Tax It)

Federal and state income tax policies clearly promote and subsidize home ownership. Your mortgage interest (most of your payment in the early years of your loan) and property taxes, for example, are fully deductible items. For the first-time buyer who has not been able to itemize deductions on income taxes, this opens entire new vistas of opportunity.

There are several excellent economic and societal reasons for this preferential treatment. First, if you would like a practical example of what a dramatic, positive impact the building and real estate industry have on the economy, visit a new subdivision under construction. You will likely have difficulty just navigating through the vehicles of tradespeople, such as electricians, plumbers and carpenters, as well as suppliers delivering lumber, fixtures and assorted amenities. You will also see a variety of real estate agents escorting buyers who are anxious and willing to commit themselves to decades of debt and monthly payments for the privilege of buying the product.

Second, homeowners generally make great citizens. They pay their property taxes (albeit sometimes grudgingly); they join local service organizations; and rarely do they torch their neighborhood, no matter how disgruntled they become over a particular governmental policy or how excited they become over their favorite athletic team winning or losing a national championship.

Now for the bad news. Local governments need money to operate, and real estate provides an incredible resource for them. Two economic characteristics make real estate irresistible to tax collectors: (1) it's unique and (2) it's immobile. Every piece of real estate in America is identifiable by its own legal description. No two are alike, even if they are side by side in the same subdivision. And real property is stationary. No matter how clever or creative a property owner may be, there's no hiding that taxable asset. Add to this the fact that real estate typically appreciates in value each year, and you can understand why it is the object of such admiration among tax assessors and collectors.

That can prove to be a problem for the homeowner, since it means that your property taxes will probably go up each year. That's not too bad if your income is keeping pace with inflation, but you've got a problem if you live on a fixed income. In some instances elderly taxpayers have literally been taxed out of their homes. Taxpayer revolts in California and elsewhere have blunted the onslaught somewhat; but if you decide to become a homeowner, you will likely agree with those who maintain that although they willingly accept the obligation of supporting their local government, they would welcome the opportunity to share the privilege a bit more equitably with other citizens.

The Pros Have It!

Okay, I admit it. I've given myself an easy argument to win, and I am biased. Although there are certainly situations where renting is the wiser alternative, home ownership is clearly the choice most of us would opt for, assuming we could afford it. But before we take a look at the specific steps involved in the process, let's talk about overall strategy and tactics.

Get Smart: Homebuying Strategy and Tactics

As you pursue your homebuying dream, it is wise to have both a disciplined plan of attack and a general philosophy to guide you. I will be expanding upon many of these topics as we progress, but here's an overview of what I suggest.

••13••••••••••••••••••••••••••••••••••

Your Lucky 13 Homebuying Survival Strategies

1. Learn as much as you possibly can about the entire process on your own.

You've heard it before and it's true. You will likely never make a larger monetary investment than the one you make in your home. If that doesn't get your attention, consider the obvious fact that you, and your family if you have one, will have to live in it, probably for several years. That should motivate you to become very well informed. At a minimum, I hope you will study the information in this book very carefully.

You will probably want to do additional research. For example, let's say that after reading the information on credit, you follow my suggestion, get a copy of your credit report and discover you have a problem you didn't realize you had. It is likely you will have to do additional digging to get the specific guidance you need. I've included a bibliography of what I consider the best books on the market that relate to homebuying. One of my more enjoyable jobs is book review editor for *Real Estate Professional* magazine, so I've reviewed each of the books I include. To keep current, read the real estate sections of large metropolitan newspapers. They are typically published on Sunday and contain topical information that will be helpful. If you are near a community college, there usually are excellent real estate courses available, sometimes on the specific subject of homebuying. Be aware, however, that these courses are often conducted by real estate agents who are looking for customers, so be a discriminating participant.

2. Get help from competent professionals at every step.

I'll have specific guidance for you on how to choose a real estate agent and an attorney as well as other professionals. Some of this help will cost you money, while much of it will be free. Some of these people will represent others in the transaction, while some will represent you. Others will be neutral. You can still get invaluable services from all of them. Please *do not* jump into house hunting until you have read and thoroughly understand the material on how real estate agents operate and who represents whom in a transaction.

3. *Know how to evaluate information and advice.*

One of your most important tasks will be to gather information with the diligence of an FBI agent. You also need to do the same thing an FBI agent does—namely, evaluate the credibility of the source of the information. For example, let's say you ask a real estate broker if it's a good time to buy a home. For the real estate broker it's *always* a good time for you to buy a home. Or let's say you ask a real estate broker who specializes in what we call buyer brokerage if it makes sense for buyers to hire their own agent to represent them as opposed to relying on the traditional method of working exclusively with agents who represent the seller. It's not hard to guess what the response will be. This is not to say the advice you get from these folks may not be valuable. Just identify whatever vested interest is present.

4. *Make a list—check it twice.*

On important items, always double-check information you are given with another source. You will need to be discreet, of course, but you must verify critically important matters. For example, if the owner of a piece of land on which you plan to build your dream home tells you that it has been approved for the installation of a septic system, check with the local governmental approval authority to verify that it has, and for what size home.

5. *Know your strengths and share that knowledge with sellers.*

Homebuying is an emotional process, but then so is homeselling. People become emotionally attached to their homes, some a great deal more than others. In ideal circumstances most people want to sell their homes for a fair price to those who will give them the tender, loving care they deserve. So if you come across as a serious, qualified buyer who fills that bill, the chances are it will give you an edge in the negotiation process.

6. *Don't fall in love.*

As you are shopping for a home, it is quite likely you will find at least one or two that really appeal to you—i.e., that you could get emotional about owning. The problem is that when we fall in love it becomes apparent to everyone.

7. If you do fall in love, don't show it.

If, despite your best efforts, you can't help falling in love with a particular home, at least try to conceal it. While you want the sellers to know you appreciate their home and will take great care of it, you don't want it to be obvious that you've fallen head over heels. If you do, it will not help your negotiating position.

8. Hide your hot buttons.

In any buying situation most of us have our hot buttons—specific things that really turn us on and cause us to say "I'll take it!" and perhaps irrationally disregard other important information. (I had a student once whose hot button was floors. He almost made a very unwise investment in a hardware store because the wooden, hand-crafted floors turned him on.) Your first step is one of self-analysis. Know what your hot buttons are, but do not share that information with those who might use the information against you. Above all, if your hot button inadvertently gets pushed during a house-hunting trip, see strategy #7.

9. Be a reasonable but resolute participant in the entire process—and look out for number one!

Based upon what I observed while selling real estate and my own experiences as a consumer, I am thoroughly convinced that the best transactions are those in which everyone achieves their major goals—the win-win philosophy. In the ideal scenario you will find the well-kept and structurally sound home of your dreams, bargain in good faith, pay a reasonable price and live in it happily ever after or until you decide to sell it, whichever occurs first. You already know that it doesn't always work that way in the real world and, sadly, not everyone plays by the golden rule. What might strike you as criminal activity may be looked upon by someone else as normal business or aggressive marketing. That being the case, while you do not want to take unfair or illegal advantage of anyone (for your own ultimate welfare, if for no other reason), you do want to vigilantly look out for your own interests at every step.

Don't be intimidated by anyone, and never be reluctant to ask questions. There is truly no such thing as a dumb question. Remember that it is your hard-earned money that is fueling the entire process. Don't be reluctant to ask the tough or sensitive questions because you are afraid you will embarrass someone.

10. Always know a whole lot more about what's going on than the other folks involved in the process think you know.

I'm not counseling dishonesty here; I'm just suggesting that for your own best interests you play it very close to the vest. Some consumers involved in business transactions seem compelled to try to impress everyone with how knowledgeable they are, often to their disadvantage.

11. Ask questions you already know the answer to.

Dirty pool, you say? Not really. It's actually quite an effective technique. I know, as I've had it used on me—probably more often than I realized. I'm sure it happened when I listed a home of a lady who, a few years earlier, had been a very successful REALTOR® in another state. She didn't share that information with me until we had listed her property, located a buyer, negotiated the sale and were about to close the transaction. I remember being impressed by the variety of probing questions she asked. I assume I passed her unannounced, ongoing pop quizzes and veracity checks, since she remained friendly and cooperative throughout.

12. Establish a paper trail.

Keep a copy of everything, including such things as offers to purchase, inspection reports, property disclosures, loan applications, title reports and appraisals. If any disputes ever arise over who said what, when and to whom, those with a written record are always one up on those without one. Keep accurate records of all improvements you make on your home, for that will be of critical importance when it is time to sell and you are (hopefully) figuring out how much tax you will have to pay on your capital gains. It will be more convenient if you keep your written records in one large file.

13. Keep a positive attitude—and persevere!

It will be easy to get discouraged, particularly if you are trying to figure out how to finance your first home or that more expensive move-up in the suburbs. You may even get further down in the dumps when you realize that a mutation of Murphy's law is at work: it will always cost more and take longer than you had planned. Keep your goal in sight, get your priorities straight, maintain your sense of humor and persevere!

2

▼

Hunkering Down

Whether buying your home turns out to be the American Dream come true or the *Nightmare on Elm Street* will depend to a great extent upon how well informed you are and how you conduct your homebuying campaign. Doing it right involves some very basic, but absolutely essential, steps. They are as follows: (1) determining where you are now, (2) deciding where you want to be and (3) developing a strategy to get there.

Hunkering-Down Strategy

As a young air force officer, I was stationed in Alabama when legendary football coach Bear Bryant was at the University of Alabama. Each Sunday afternoon during football season I, along with the rest of the state, watched on TV as the Bear narrated the Crimson Tide's game from the previous day. On those rare occasions when the Tide lost, or didn't win as impressively as some thought they should have, Bear was invariably asked what happened. His response typically was to growl, "That was the sorriest job of coaching I've ever seen. We've just got to suck it up and hunker down."

That philosophy made a lasting impression on me. First, don't blame others for your problems, no matter how much they may deserve it.

Second, stop whining and start working on the problem. In football, life or buying a house, it's a valuable strategy, if not always the easiest to follow. When getting the resources together to buy a home, it may take a whole lot of sucking up and hunkering down.

Where You Are Now

No matter what your home dreams may be, as a matter of practical reality you have to know how much home you can realistically afford and the likelihood that a lender will agree with your assessment and make you a loan. If money is no object, you can skip this section.

The Balance Sheet

Your best bet is to look at your financial and credit situation through the eyes of a potential lender. That means that you must determine your net worth first. Don't get scared off; it's not that tough. Even if the news is bad, it's better to face the situation realistically and decide what you need to do to improve it.

Swing by any financial institution and simply ask the receptionist for a real estate loan application. There's no need to get involved in any lengthy discussions at this stage. You just want a copy of the form for your worksheet. All forms ask for basically the same information. For now, what you need is a rough analysis for your own reference. That should entail completing the information on employment, monthly income and housing expenses, and assets and liabilities. At some point you will have to sit down across the desk from a no-nonsense, steely eyed mortgage loan officer and go through the same exercise, so you may as well get your stuff together now to give you a good preview of what's coming.

Whether the news is good or bad, you have to know. And there is no point in embellishing or neglecting to include certain unpleasant information you would rather forget. Even if honesty were not the best policy, eventually everything you put down (or fail to put down, if it's relevant) will be checked with about the same thoroughness as an FBI investigation of a Supreme Court nominee, so you may as well tell it exactly like it is.

Your Credit Status

If you were loaning someone, let's say, a hundred thousand dollars and giving them 30 years to pay it back, how thoroughly would you check that person out? My guess is that you would do some pretty serious investigating. Mortgage lenders do very serious investigating. Even if they are not inclined to do that, they "package" most of the loans they make and sell them (literally) in what is known as the secondary mortgage market. When they do that, they generate more money to make other loans, collect fees and thereby ensure that they stay profitable and in business. That being the case, they are very careful to ensure that the loans they make will meet the precise and rigid standards that must be met before Ginnie Mae, Fannie Mae or Freddie Mac will buy them. (These are the common names for the three largest purchasers of mortgages in the secondary market.)

The fancy word for the whole process is *underwriting,* which simply means an assessment of the risk involved in loaning you the money. Long, hard experience has shown that the single best indicator of how likely a person is to repay a loan is their past performance in repaying other obligations—i.e., their credit history. Income is important, but one's track record is critical. For that reason, you must know exactly what your credit record reflects. If there are errors, you need to correct them. If there are past problems, you must try to compensate for them. Here are some specific suggestions in each area.

Check It Out.   You can order a copy of your credit report by contacting one of the credit reporting agencies. There are the "big three" national agencies, whose addresses follow and a wide array of local and regional organizations.

Now you can start doing preliminary contact work with a mortgage loan officer at a local lending institution. Ask who handles their credit reporting and how one goes about ordering a credit report. You will get a good initial impression of how helpful and responsive that lender is likely to be when you actually get down to the business of borrowing money. If they know you are a prospective customer, common sense indicates that they will be as cooperative and responsive as possible.

Another course of action is to look under "credit reporting agencies" or "credit bureaus" in the yellow pages of your local phone directory. Call their offices and ask for the cost and procedures involved in getting your report. It will take a written request and will probably cost between $10 and $20.

Each of the "big three" national credit reporting agencies has a consumer assistance office with a toll-free number. It is a good idea to call each agency to check for their latest information and for your general education.

- TRW Credit Data Division
  National Consumer Relations Center
  P.O. Box 749029
  Dallas, TX 75374-9029
  800-682-7654

- Trans Union
  Consumer Relations Center
  P.O. Box 7000
  North Olmsted, OH 44070-7000
  800-521-4019

- Equifax (CBI in some localities)
  Office of Consumer Affairs
  P.O. Box 740241
  Atlanta, GA 30374
  800-685-1111

At the present time, TRW will provide one free credit report per year. Call their toll-free number for instructions. Don't be surprised if it takes you a while to get your report. I followed their instructions precisely, but it took me three trys to convince them that I was, in fact, a real person with a credit history. To be honest, the report I finally received didn't make all that much sense to me, but I suppose if there had been a glaring problem it would have been apparent.

While the credit report you get on yourself from one of the credit agencies will be useful, it will not be as complete as the one the lending institution orders when you actually apply for a loan. You will also have to pay for that one.

Clear It Up. The purpose of this whole exercise is to let you know if you have a credit problem. My guess is that you already know that, but you've got to see what the official record says since lending decisions will be based upon your record. Even though you may think your record is spotless, mistakes do occur.

If you have the words *junior* or *senior* after your name or have a very common name, the probability of error increases. For example, my son is a junior (my wife insisted). When he applied for a loan, they got our credit files mixed. He said he was asked how he had managed to amass so much debt in such a short life. Problems such as that are fairly easy to correct, although you need to work directly with the credit reporting company in writing and you must be persistent. If there are inappropriate entries on your credit report caused by an ex-spouse who was, or is, a loose cannon, you will have more of a problem and may need to seek some legal help.

You will have even more of a challenge if you've had actual credit problems yourself. After ensuring that the report reflects the true situation, your best course of action is to prove by more recent actions that you are now a solid, debt-paying citizen. If you've never bought anything on credit, you need to get a few credit accounts and keep them current. There are several major credit cards that charge no annual fee and actually pay you a dividend based upon your charges. This is only a good deal if you pay total amounts as due monthly and avoid interest charges. For further guidance on solving credit problems, I recommend you refer to the book *The Credit Repair Kit* by attorney John Ventura. (See the Bibliography.) It's clear, concise and focuses on the typical problems borrowers face.

Final Countdown

After you've done your income, asset and credit analysis, you will have the information needed to estimate how much house you can afford and the probability that you will get a loan. I recommend that you first do your own calculations, using the information that follows, and then I suggest you call in a professional—a loan officer at a lending institution. That institution can be a commercial bank, a savings and loan, a credit union, a mortgage banker or a mortgage broker.

Self-Analysis.   How much house you can buy will be determined by the amount of money you have to put down and the size of the loan for which you can qualify. Lacking that information, there is a good chance that you will waste your time and everyone else's. *Qualify* is the key word.

Here's basically how it goes. You will have compiled the information you need to do this when you were constructing your balance sheet that we discussed earlier:

- *Gross income.* This is simply your total income from all sources, before taxes.

- *Net income.* You get this by totaling up your monthly debts (a sobering experience) and subtracting it from your gross income.

- *Qualifying ratios.* These numbers reflect the relationship between a borrower's gross and net income and proposed mortgage debt. The precise ratios lenders use vary from time to time and from loan program to loan program, but 28 percent and 36 percent are common.

Here's what that means. When you buy a home and get a mortgage, you join that select group of citizens to whom the term PITI has significance. PITI stands for principal, interest, taxes, insurance. A few other items may creep in, such as private mortgage insurance and homeowners' association fees. The total figure represents your monthly housing payment. A 28 percent ratio means that your monthly housing payment cannot exceed 28 percent of your gross income.

For example, your gross annual income is $45,000, for a monthly income of $3,750. You buy a $120,000 home, with $20,000 down, and get a $100,000, 30-year fixed-rate loan at 7 percent. Your monthly principal and interest (PI) is $665. We will estimate property tax (T) at $150 and insurance (I) at $30. Your PITI thus totals $845. That represents about 23 percent of your gross monthly income ($845 divided by $3,750). You qualify, since 28 percent of your monthly gross (the maximum) is $1,050. The good news is that you've cleared the first hurdle—affectionately known as the front-end qualifying ratio. Furthermore, you get a chance to clear another hurdle—the back-end qualifying ratio. You must make it over both hurdles to get the loan.

To compute this, you compile all your monthly debts (please don't tell me you have two car payments) and add them to your projected monthly housing payment (the infamous PITI). Assume your monthly debt load is $400. Add that to your PITI of $845 and the total is $1,245.

You make it over this hurdle, too, since your ratio is 33 percent ($1,245 divided by $3,750) and the back-end qualifying ratio is 36 percent.

I am certain that all of this is perfectly clear to you and that you have no questions, but in the event that you may need a little further guidance, here's what I suggest. It is obvious that to perform the analysis, you must have a specific loan amount in mind and know the term and the mortgage rate, which has an aggravating habit of changing almost daily. As I am sure you also recognize, when rates go down you can qualify for a larger loan. When they go up, unfortunately, the opposite is true.

If you like to crunch numbers yourself, buy an inexpensive calculator that does loan amortization calculations. In short order, with nothing more than the instructional manual, you should be able to figure out all the possibilities. Or you can do your calculations the easy way by cultivating a good source at a local lending institution and having them do the whole thing for you. It is always preferable, however, to be an informed participant. Since I am sure you now fit into that category, it's time to venture further out into the real world.

Professional Help.   Based on your contacts up to this point, tentatively decide where you would like to apply for your loan. You can get rate comparisons from quote sheets in the real estate sections of newspapers, from real estate agents or by calling around.

A quick word here about the mortgage interest rates that you will see quoted. Lenders are required to include the APR, or annual percentage rate. That must be computed by a standard formula and will incorporate charges other than the actual interest rate charged for the money. After all the hoopla, that's the figure you should use to compare rates.

When you talk to the mortgage loan officer, indicate that you want to arrange a prequalification interview. That's becoming a standard service that lenders perform, generally at no cost. Their motivation is to secure customers, since they make money lending money—to good risks.

At the interview the lender will simply use the income and asset information you provide and will do an analysis of how much you are likely to borrow, using current interest rates and applying them to basic mortgage loan options, such as fixed and adjustable rates. It is important for you to understand that the prequalification interview does not commit you or the lender. If you are not satisfied in any way, you are under no obligation. On the other hand, if the information you provide is faulty or incomplete, your credit doesn't later check out or mortgage interest rates escalate rapidly, all bets are off. If you understand that, it is still a valuable procedure and I highly recommend that you do it.

Mortgage brokers can perform the same service. They arrange for loans, as opposed to actually making them. Their fees typically are paid by the lenders, since they do much of the lender's work. But this is not always true, so ask specifically if there is a charge for their services. If you can get a loan more cheaply by going directly to the lender, do so. The advantage mortgage brokers have is that they have access to a wide variety of lenders (although not all) and are familiar with the different types of loans offered. Mortgage bankers do essentially the same thing, but they sometimes loan the money themselves.

If you want to go one step further, some lending institutions will process you for an actual preapproved loan. This will cost you some money, since there will be a credit report involved, but you will then know the amount of the loan for which you could qualify. You are then a much stronger purchaser in the eyes of the seller, since there is no financing contingency in your offer to purchase. The way it works is you get the preapproved loan for a certain amount of money and then shop for a home. These approvals are for a specific period of time and will have several caveats, including that if you mess up your credit, you are no longer approved.

Deciding Where You Want To Be

This may not be too tough for you. After you do the preliminary work, you will know roughly how much home you can afford. It may simply be a matter of deciding that you are going to buy the best house you can, without jeopardizing your economic future. If you can afford a lot more home than you think you need, it will simply be a happy matter of sifting out options and selecting the one that makes the most sense for you.

Developing a Financial Strategy To Get There

Unfortunately, there often is a monetary gap between where you are and where you want to be. It will come as no big surprise that getting the money together for a down payment is usually the single biggest hurdle, assuming you have the income and credit necessary to qualify for the loan. There are only a few viable options, none of which are the type of advice we like to hear. Nonetheless, here they are.

You've Got To Spend Less

You need to reduce this to hard figures. That means you must establish a budget. (I know, I hate it, too.) To do this, you must know exactly how you are spending your money. It will require a little research, but it shouldn't be too tough to determine. Hopefully, you will have what is called *discretionary income*, or money above and beyond what you need for your basic shelter, utilities and such expenses as life insurance. How you spend or save your discretionary income is a matter of priorities. If you are considering a two-week vacation that will cost a few thousand dollars, consider a less expensive option or simply defer it. Above all, avoid big-ticket items, such as automobiles. Coax a few thousand more miles out of the old clunker if at all possible. Automobile loans are cited by mortgage loan officers as one of the single most important reasons people fail to qualify for mortgages. And finally, and here I'm really messing into your private life, avoid eating out as much as possible. I know that's tough advice to follow, particularly for those who don't have a stay-at-home partner to fix the meals, but it's an incredible expense, even if your tastes run to pizza and hamburgers. Consider the favor you will be doing your arteries by not plugging them up with fat, and it's a winning strategy all the way around.

You've Got To Save More

This doesn't get any easier, does it? The most effective way of saving is to pay yourself first. That means putting part of your salary away before you ever see it and forgetting (figuratively) that it's there. Most of us spend what we earn. It is remarkable how that works, no matter how much we earn. If you never see the money, the chances are better that you will not come to depend upon it, although you will have to resist the temptation to dip into it for what you rationalize are absolutely essential items. Where should you put this money? Since you are hopefully looking at an accumulation phase of a year or so at the maximum, deposit it in a place you can get at quickly and where your principal is safe. Depending upon interest rates, that could mean certificates of deposit (CDs) or certain money market funds.

If All Else Fails

If you can't spend less or save more, then your most immediate other practical option is to earn more. That may mean an extra, part-time job for you (and/or your mate) or a higher-paying job. That strategy may even entail some risk, since lenders are wary of people who have just taken new jobs and do not have a track record. We will examine a few other possibilities in our discussion on financing (such as rich relative cosigners and investor partners), but the spend-less, save-more strategy is the most practical—if not the most popular.

Getting To Know the Players

To this point I've suggested that you do a lot of studying and self-analysis but that you make personal contact with only one individual, a loan officer or mortgage broker to help you with financing questions. Before you actually start talking to real estate agents and begin your serious home search, you must know who the principal players are and exactly where each is coming from.

Red Flag Checklist and Survival Strategies

The term *red flag* has become very popular in the real estate profession. If an item or a situation is described as red flag, it simply means that it warrants your very close attention. It's basically an alert to watch your backside. Although it may turn out to be nothing at all, it could indicate that something has gone terribly wrong, or is about to go wrong. In any event you need to investigate. A big brown stain on the ceiling, for example, is definitely a red flag. A real estate agent who never looks you in the eye may even qualify. With each red flag we will list a suggested strategy for survival.

1. You see a shiny red BMW at the car dealer's showroom and decide you can't live without it.

Strategy: Resist the temptation. Car payments are one of the most common reasons folks don't qualify for a home loan. Drive the Edsel for a few more years.

2. You watch an old episode of "Love Boat" and decide you and your mate absolutely must take that cruise to Pango Pango.

Strategy: See number 1 above. It's a matter of priorities. Besides, Pango Pango is highly overrated.

3. In totaling up your net worth, you come up with a negative figure.

Strategy: Bad sign, but at least you know where you stand. You only have two practical options: cut expenses and/or increase income.

4. You are denied credit for a department store credit card.

Strategy: If you have not done so, check your credit status immediately. The Federal Fair Credit Reporting Act gives you the right to a free copy of your credit report if you are denied credit based on credit record information. You must do this within 30 days. If there are errors, correct them.

5. You get sick to your stomach when you drive by a house and see someone mowing the lawn.

Strategy: Better do a reality check. Homes demand care. If you and/or your mate are not emotionally equipped for the responsibilities of home ownership, renting is an entirely honorable option.

6. Your employer has indicated that the chances are excellent that you will be transferred to the opposite side of the continent within the next year.

Strategy: It's probably not a good idea to consider buying unless you plan to be in the area for at least three years. Some say two years, but that depends upon how hot the real estate market is—and remains—while you are there.

7. When you proudly inform the loan officer during your prequalification interview that you are successfully self-employed, she doesn't seem as impressed as you thought she should be.

Strategy: Here's the problem. Mortgage delinquency rates for self-employed individuals are unusually high. You will be required to submit additional documentation, including your federal income tax returns for the past several years. It's not the kiss of death—it will just require more hunkering down.

8. The mortgage loan officer who does your prequalification interview spends only 30 seconds in asking questions before announcing that you are qualified for twice as much mortgage as your own analysis indicated.

Strategy: Double-check these numbers with another loan officer at another lending institution. It is highly unlikely that you were that far off.

9. When you ask the mortgage loan officer how long it will take to get your loan approved, the answer is, "Assuming everything goes right, about 45 days."

Strategy: Murphy was an optimist. Anticipate what may go wrong and attempt to head it off. Don't make any unalterable plans based on a best-case scenario.

10. The only home it looks as though you can afford is an 87-mile commute to your job, one-way.

Strategy: For most of us that is too long a commute, which means that the homebuying decision needs to be postponed until resources more nearly match needs.

3

······▼······

Getting To Know the
Cast of Characters

It is entirely possible, in theory anyhow, for you to buy a home without many people getting involved. Just find a property that's for sale, pay cash for it, get a deed and move in. So much for theory. In the real world almost all home sales involve several players in addition to buyers and sellers. It is imperative that you know who does what, who works for whom and what motivates each party involved. We will look at the leading players in this chapter and the supporting cast in Chapter 4.

Some of this material will seem confusing to you. That's because it is! But stay with me. Once you are familiar with the basics you will be able to operate with confidence, and my guess is that you will be better informed than any of the other participants. In this chapter we will cover the fundamental roles and functions of each participant. We will discuss each player in the context of the actual homebuying process.

Real Estate Agents

Why do most homeowners use real estate agents to sell the homestead? There are several reasons. First, selling a home is a complex matter involving pricing, marketing, financing and an often bewildering array of administrative details. A competent real estate agent can efficiently take care of many of these matters personally and can assure that the remaining details are done by other qualified professionals. Why do homebuyers use real estate agents? Simple. They have to, unless they buy directly from one of the very small minority of homeowners who sell without an agent. (We will discuss this in Chapter 4.) That being the case, you need to know how the system works.

The Basics

All real estate agents are required to be licensed by the state in which they sell. Licensees fall into three categories: (1) salespeople, (2) associate brokers and (3) brokers. Salespeople are the most numerous; it's the first step on the ladder. All states require that prospective licensees pass an objective, written examination. Almost all require formal classroom training. Associate brokers are those with additional experience but who work for a broker. The broker is in charge and is responsible for the entire operation. The first time you come in contact with a real estate agent, ask for a business card. State regulations require the person's licensing category be indicated on it.

Brokerage firms are organized as corporations, partnerships or proprietorships. Some are members of national franchises, while others are independent. The legal organization or franchise status is not important to you. What is important for you to know is that if you have difficulty in working with a salesperson or an associate broker and cannot resolve the problem to your satisfaction, your next stop should be with the broker. All salespeople and associate brokers work under the direct, continuing supervision of the broker for as long as they are affiliated with that firm. All transactions—sales and listings—are actually entered into in the name of the broker. You may never even meet the broker, but that's who is in charge and responsible, nonetheless.

If you can't get satisfaction from the broker, your next step is the state real estate commission. These commissions are called by different names in different states, but all states have one agency responsible for protecting consumers' interests by supervising and regulating professional real estate activities within the state. They conduct investigations, perform inspections and hand out disciplinary actions when appropriate.

How Do REALTORS® Fit into the Equation?

To many people REALTOR® and real estate agent are synonymous terms, much to the understandable dismay of REALTORS®. The word REALTOR® is a registered trade name that may only be used by members affiliated with the National Association of REALTORS®. Roughly half of all real estate licensees in the United States are REALTORS®. One distinguishing characteristic of REALTORS® is that members subscribe to an elaborate code of professional ethics. Another is the wide variety of professional education courses they offer. You will note that in the chapters that follow, I use REALTOR® and agent interchangeably. That's because I'm going to suggest that the agent you work with be a REALTOR®.

Enter Buyers and Sellers

Whom do real estate agents represent? This gets a little tricky, but hang in there because it is very important. Here is an example of how the system has worked for years—and it is still by far the most common arrangement.

● ●

Standard Fare: Seller Agency

Widow Wanda Wiggs lists her home on Harmony Lane in River City with salesperson Lance LeBow. LeBow works for broker Sarah Saintly at Golden Rule Realty, an independent real estate brokerage also located in River City and operated by Saintly as a sole proprietorship. All Golden Rule licensees are REALTORS®. Wiggs authorizes Saintly to put the listing on the Multiple Listing Service (MLS), a marketing device that gets the listing wide exposure. Widow Wiggs has employed Broker Saintly to market her home. The listing is actually an employment contract. Broker Saintly is Widow Wiggs's agent. An agent is authorized to act for and represent another person, called the principal or client. An agent (Saintly) owes a fiduciary responsibility to the principal (Wiggs). In essence that means that the interests of Wiggs are to be placed above everyone else's in the transaction. Salesperson LeBow is a subagent of Wiggs (since he works for, and is an agent of, the primary agent, Saintly) and has a fiduciary responsibility to Wiggs. Wiggs agrees to pay Saintly a brokerage fee (typically, a percent of the selling price) when Saintly produces a ready, willing and able buyer. It's an exclusive-right-to-sell listing, which means that no matter who sells the property (including Wiggs), Saintly has earned a commission. When Saintly put the listing on the MLS, there was what is called a unilateral offer of subagency made to the other real estate licensees who are members. That simply means other licensees can market the property by agreeing also to be a subagent of Wiggs and accept that fiduciary responsibility. In a fee-splitting arrangement (which Wiggs must authorize), they share the brokerage fee if they produce that coveted ready, willing and able buyer.

● ●

I assume you detect a common thread in all of this. Everyone is representing the Widow Wiggs and putting her interests first. Who, you may ask, represents the buyer in this scenario? In a legal sense, no one. What obligations, if any, do the licensees have to the buyer? Basically, honesty and disclosure of material facts. Books have been written on what constitutes a material fact, but it essentially means anything that influences a person's homebuying decision.

The Real World

There are some difficulties with seller agency. One of the problems is that things are not always so neat and tidy when we enter the actual marketplace. Note that the seller agency system as I've described it might imply an adversarial relationship between seller and buyer, with all the heavyweights in the seller's corner. In the real world, treating buyers as adversaries is not how real estate agents survive and prosper. First, and most important, unless buyers perceive that they are being treated fairly and honestly, there will be no sale. Furthermore, the real estate agent will get no telephone call when that buyer later becomes a seller. You can see that there is a certain amount of potential for confusion in the system. Here's an example.

●●●

Seller Agency in River City

Lotta Cashette, a single mother, has decided to relocate from her present residence in Gotham to tranquil River City. She writes the chamber of commerce for information about real estate. An enterprising real estate agent from Golden Rule Realty, Lance LeBow, calls her to offer help. Lotta likes what she hears and agrees to work with Lance. He meets her at the airport when she visits on a house-hunting trip. He makes reservations for her at a motel. He takes her out to dinner. He's friendly. He's professional. He knows his business. He finds the perfect house, owned by a nice grandmotherly type, the Widow Wiggs. As a matter of fact, he listed the house and knows everything about it. He helps Lotta write up the offer and even suggests an offering price of $5,000 below the listed price. He presents it to Wiggs. It's accepted on the spot. He arranges for a structural and pest inspection. He lines up financing. He even goes to the bank with Lotta to make the loan application. He attends the closing and presents her with the keys to her new home along with a dozen long-stem red roses. They embrace. Lance begins to look a lot like Tom Selleck to Lotta.

Question: Who was Lance legally supposed to be representing in this transaction? *Answer:* The Widow Wiggs. *Question:* Who do you believe Lotta thought was representing her in this transaction? *Answer:* Lance.

●●●

In the majority of homebuying situations, research shows that buyers think the agent they work with represents them, when in fact that is not the case. Is that a problem? It could be. Let's say that Lotta told Lance that she would offer $92,000 for the house but would go to the full asking price of $97,000 if she had to. Lance's fiduciary responsibility to Wiggs would dictate that he pass that information on. You can see why it is very important that as a homebuyer you know exactly who is representing whom and act accordingly.

It's quite possible that Lotta is supremely happy in her little home on Harmony Lane and recommends Lance to all her friends and acquaintances. On the other hand . . .

• •

Trouble in River City

Let's say things go sour for Lotta after she moves in. She finds that the large handmade throw rug that the Widow Wiggs generously left in the guest bedroom covers rotting boards that give way and swallow her overweight poodle. When she turns on her clothes dryer, all the lights in the neighborhood go out. Her little Egbert can't go to the school down the block because it is being closed for budgetary reasons, and he will have to be bused across town where students must go through metal detectors before they can enter the building. She discovers the house next door is owned by the drummer in a punk rock band, and he frequently practices into the wee hours. Lotta would understandably have tight jaws. She could become so upset that she might see an attorney. Skilled in the ways of agency as it relates to real estate, the attorney would probably ask Lotta if she thought Lance was representing her. Of course Lotta thought Lance represented her. Her narrative convinces the attorney, the attorney's narrative convinces a judge and Lance and his broker, as well as the Widow Wiggs, are undoubtedly in big trouble.

Lance entered into what is known as an undisclosed dual agency. In other words, in practicality he actually was representing both Lotta and Wiggs without proper authorization. That's all the attorney had to prove. There might be a recision of contract. There may be monetary damages. Lance and Sarah might be in trouble with the real estate commissioner.

• •

Is there a way a buyer can have representation in the homebuying process and even things up a bit? Yes. It's called buyer agency.

• •

Buyer Agency: Another Option

Lotta receives several calls from enterprising REALTORS®as a result of her letter to the River City Chamber of Commerce about her impending move. One of them, broker Abby Lincoln of Emancipation Realty, explains in brief and convincing fashion a concept called buyer agency. If Lotta will sign a contract authorizing Abby to represent her, she will then be Lotta's agent and owe her the fiduciary responsibilities. Lotta likes the idea but asks who pays. Abby says she is confident she can work out an arrangement with the listing broker in which the commission from the seller will cover the fee, so it will cost Lotta nothing. Lotta likes that idea even more. Abby meets Lotta at the airport and Lotta signs a contract employing Abby to represent her. When Abby calls any broker with a listing on the MLS, she informs that broker that she is representing a buyer, rejects that unilateral offer of subagency and works out the details of the fee splitting. If that gets settled to everyone's satisfaction, then we will have a buyer's agent representing the buyer and a seller's agent representing the seller.

• •

There is a third possibility. It's called disclosed dual agency.

• •

Disclosed Dual Agency: Serving Two Masters

When Lotta gets that phone call, it's from Lance. After hearing her needs, Lance says his office has a listing that he thinks will be perfect for Lotta. He explains the whole agency concept and the alternatives available. He suggests that his brokerage could represent both parties—a disclosed dual agency. Most states permit dual agency if both parties give their informed consent, but common law and state administrative rules clearly favor the single agency concept.

• •

Identity Crisis

There are many informed real estate professionals and legal scholars who maintain agency law is not appropriate to real estate. As the profession has developed, the emphasis has been on making sure everyone in the transaction is satisfied, not on acting as an advocate of one party. There is no question that a severe identity crisis has developed. As the situation has become more muddled, state legislatures have begun to step into the breach.

State Laws

California was one of the first to try to clarify things by passing a law that requires agency disclosure. As a matter of fact, in most matters that relate to real estate you can look to California to see the future. They have so many transactions there that anything that can go wrong has, it has resulted in a lawsuit, an appeal has been made and acted upon by the Supreme Court and the whole thing has been made into a TV miniseries. Regarding agency, the following is what California's law requires be disclosed. They've done a good job of reducing things to the basics. What you may conclude, however, is that there doesn't seem to be a lot of difference among your choices.

Real Estate Agency Relationship
(As required by the Civil Code, State of California)

When you enter into a discussion with a real estate agent regarding a real estate transaction, you should from the outset understand what type of agency relationship or representation you wish to have with the agent in the transaction.

Seller's Agent

A Seller's agent under a listing agreement with the Seller acts as the agent for the Seller only. A Seller's agent or a subagent of that agent has the following affirmative obligations:

To the Seller:

(a) A fiduciary duty of utmost care, integrity, honesty and loyalty in dealings with the Seller.

To the Buyer and the Seller:

(a) Diligent exercise of reasonable skill and care in performance of the agent's duties.

(b) A duty of honest and fair dealing and good faith.

(c) A duty to disclose all facts known to the agent materially affecting value or desirability of the property that are not known to, or within the diligent attention and observation of, the parties.

An agent is not obligated to reveal to either party any confidential information obtained from the other party which does not involve the affirmative duties set forth above.

Buyer's Agent

A selling agent can, with a buyer's consent, agree to act as agent for the Buyer only. In these situations, the agent is not the Seller's agent, even if by agreement the agent may receive compensation for services rendered, either in full or part from the Seller. An agent acting only for a buyer has the following affirmative obligations:

To the Buyer:

(a) A fiduciary duty of utmost care, integrity, honesty and loyalty in dealings with the Buyer.

To the Buyer and the Seller:

(a) Diligent exercise of reasonable skill and care in performance of the agent's duties.

(b) A duty of honest and fair dealing and good faith.

(c) A duty to disclose all facts known to the agent materially affecting the value or desirability of the property that are not known to, or within the diligent attention and observation of, the parties.

An agent is not obligated to reveal to either party any confidential information obtained from the other party which does not involve the affirmative duties set forth above.

Agent Representing Both Buyer and Seller

A real estate agent, either acting directly or through one or more associate licensees, can legally be the agent of both the Seller and the Buyer in a transaction, but only with the knowledge and consent of both the Seller and the Buyer.

In a dual agency situation, the agent has the following affirmative obligations to both the Seller and the Buyer.

(a) A fiduciary duty of utmost care, integrity, honesty and loyalty in dealings with either the Seller or the Buyer.

(b) Other duties to the Seller and the Buyer as stated above in their respective sections.

In representing both Seller and Buyer, the agent may not, without the express permission of the respective party, disclose to the other party that the Seller will accept a price less than the listing price or that the Buyer will pay a price greater than the price offered.

Bottom Line

If we made sex as complicated as we've managed to make agency in the homebuying process, we wouldn't have to worry about world overpopulation. How can you cut through this bewildering maze and operate within the system as it currently exists to your best advantage?

By keeping your focus on your objective and by concentrating on the basics. Here's a summary of your options.

Seller Agency Balance Sheet.   For you, the homebuyer, there is a lot to be said for operating within the traditional seller agency arrangement. It's still the one people in most parts of the country understand best, and if you know how to protect your interests, you should have no difficulty. In addition, you have the advantage of being a completely free agent with no obligation to anyone except yourself. If you don't like how you are treated by one real estate agent, you can go to another.

Here's another reason you may wish to opt for seller agency. If you know the rules and play your cards right, you can get a great deal of help and assistance from an agent who officially represents the seller. As a matter of fact, in most situations you can probably get as much help as you could from a buyer's agent. In the final analysis a real estate agent best serves the client's (seller's) interests by bringing a legitimate offer from a qualified buyer (you). If the precise offer does not satisfy the seller, it can be countered. The seller's interests are certainly not served by treating the buyer (you) as though you were an antagonist. Just remember that no one gets paid until you are satisfied, no matter who is supposed to be representing whom.

Buyer Agency Balance Sheet.   The major advantage is that you have official representation by your own agent. To get that, however, you have to sign a contractual agreement and give up your freelance status. In addition, you might run into some flak from listing brokers and sellers who haven't enthusiastically accepted the buyer agency concept. As a result, it could cut down on the number of homes you might have available to consider.

If you do decide to sign up a buyer's agent, make certain all your contractual options are explained to you in detail. Just as there are several types of listing agreements, there also are several types of buyer agency contracts. You can sign one for exclusive representation, which means that no matter whom you buy from, you owe the agent a fee. Or you can sign a contract that says you can still freelance, but if the buyer agent comes up with a property you buy, then you pay the fee. The length of the contract is also flexible.

Disclosed Dual Agency Balance Sheet.   To be honest, in most traditional real estate transactions there has been an undisclosed dual agency. That's how things have gotten done. The only difference here is that it is disclosed. In this relationship the real estate agent is considered more of a facilitator or coordinator and puts no one's interest above that of another. It's also called consensual dual agency.

Your Best Choice

I'm not trying to weasel, but I think it's far more important to select a competent REALTOR® with whom to work than it is to worry that much about the agency relationship. With what you now know, you will be able to operate very successfully in any type of agency relationship you choose. I have to admit that if I were buying a home now in most areas of the United States, I would opt for seller agency simply because it is still the one that's most accepted and I like the idea of being able to operate without signing a contract with one agent.

Buyer agency, consensual dual agency or some type of other arrangement yet to be clearly defined may eventually emerge and dominate the marketplace, so stay tuned. In the meantime don't sweat the small stuff. Get qualified, find a good REALTOR® to work with, line up a nitpicky inspector to check the merchandise out for you, keep your friendly little copy of *The Homebuyer's Survival Guide* handy and start house hunting.

Red Flag Checklist and Survival Strategies

1. Your brother-in-law sells real estate. He assures you that he can serve you best by acting as the seller's agent.

Strategy: He may be right, but this is a situation in which the seller could possibly claim a conflict of interest on the agent's part. It may be better to work with your brother-in-law as a buyer's agent. And make sure he has qualifications other than the good judgment he exhibited when he married your sister.

2. The attendant at the gas station, who sells real estate part-time, tells you he has a terrific deal for you on a fixer-upper.

Strategy: Get your homebuying advice from authoritative books and reliable, full-time real estate professionals. Get your tires checked at the gas station.

3. *A homeowner tells you that he can sell his home to you without getting a real estate agent involved, even though there is a For Sale sign of a local real estate company in the front yard.*

Strategy: The most common form of listing is called an exclusive right to sell, which means that no matter who sells it (including the owner), the broker gets paid. An exclusive agency listing permits the homeowner to sell the home without paying a commission. Check with the REALTOR® with whom you are working to determine the type of listing on the property.

4. *A real estate broker tells you that property owners in the area don't like working with buyers' brokers and frequently won't cooperate in a sale.*

Strategy: That may be true. It's not an uncommon attitude. What unquestionably is true is that the broker making the statement does not like buyers' brokers. You need to investigate further to determine the actual situation in your area.

5. *A real estate broker touting buyer agency tells you horror stories about homebuyers who have been taken advantage of by real estate agents representing sellers.*

Strategy: This is one reason some traditional brokers are not always enthusiastic about buyer brokerage. Some buyer brokers tell consumers that unless they use their services, they will get fleeced in the normal seller agency arrangement. I frankly don't respect anyone who knocks the competition.

6. *You are not impressed with the vibes you are getting from a REALTOR®, but you like the fact that he is an experienced buyer broker.*

Strategy: The longer I kick around, the more inclined I am to go with my vibes. The great thing about the free market system is that if you want a buyer's broker, there's bound to be one around with whom you are more compatible.

7. *You suggest to a buyer broker that you would like a feature written into your contract that rewards him when you pay less for a home, not more. The broker balks.*

Strategy: "Let's see now. You represent me as a buyer's broker. But the more I pay for the house, the more you make, right?" Sorry, but I can't buy that. I like the arrangement where the incentive is for me to pay less. A system that rewards a buyer broker based upon how much less than asking price I pay can be worked out.

8. Your REALTOR®, *who is the seller's agent, is giving you all sorts of help, including inside information on how desperate the seller is to sell.*

Strategy: I would gratefully accept the assistance; there's nothing wrong with that. On the alleged inside information, be very cautious and don't necessarily accept it at face value. I certainly wouldn't plug my ears if the REALTOR® gave me the information, however.

9. You want to sign on with a buyer's broker but for only one transaction. The broker responds, "The standard agreement is for 180 days."

Strategy: There is no standard agreement. You can do anything to which you both consent. Obviously, the broker would like a longer contract. Decide what you want and stick to your guns.

10. You are negotiating with a buyer's broker to represent you. He says it is customary to pay him a retainer plus an hourly fee.

Strategy: What he meant to say was that he hopes this becomes customary. Almost all buyer brokers get compensated "from the transaction," which simply means that when the deal closes, they get paid from the commission the seller agreed to pay the listing broker.

4

......▼......

Meet the Supporting Cast

As much as I admire a positive and enthusiastic attitude, there is a lot to be said for a healthy dose of well-placed pessimism concerning the buying of homes. Consider each step you take and ask yourself this question: "What can possibly go wrong here, and how can I protect myself?" Know where to go for help and study the motivations of all parties with whom you deal. Here's a rundown.

Attorneys

Custom and law vary regarding the role that attorneys play in real estate transactions. While in most areas of the country real estate brokers prepare the offers to purchase that result in contracts when accepted, there are places where this is traditionally done by attorneys. Whatever the situation may be where you live, my advice is short and to the point: Never, ever engage in any type of real estate transaction without being represented by a lawyer. There are no exceptions to this rule. You've got too much at stake, and it's not going to cost you that much, considered in the context of the entire transaction. Of course, you need to find an attorney who is competent and honest. (No, those are not mutually exclusive adjectives.)

Selecting and Working with an Attorney

Select an attorney before you start house hunting. Talk to folks and investigate. Check with lending institutions, title and escrow companies and professional organizations. You want someone who does a lot of real estate work. You don't want an attorney who has to spend hours researching the topic—at your expense. It is advisable to call a few attorneys on the phone and/or interview them personally. Ask about fees. You will probably be quoted an hourly rate that will cause temporary cardiac arrest, but it won't take long for an attorney to review a standard transaction. If there's a problem detected that could cause you major dollar trauma later, it will save you money in the long run.

You will want to confer briefly with an attorney for general guidance before you make your offer. If the seller makes any changes to your offer, make your acceptance of those changes subject to your attorney's final approval. In most instances that will not require an extensive review. You will also want to have your attorney review closing documents to ensure that your interests are properly represented and monetary prorations (what you owe, what the seller owes) are done accurately. In some parts of the country the buyer's attorney also does a title search on the property to make certain there are no title problems.

An Attention Getter

Do you know what I notice in real estate transactions when the word *attorney* is used? Everyone is a great deal more attentive to what is going on and what is said. I therefore recommend that very early in your dealings with any and all real estate agents, you casually but clearly announce, "Of course my attorney will have to review everything." That's an extremely effective move, even if you haven't selected your attorney yet. (Okay, it's effective even if you don't plan to have an attorney at all, but I don't recommend it.)

Sellers

We have discussed sellers in the context of the agency relationship, but now we need to explore the subject somewhat more deeply. If the seller is represented by a real estate agent, you will probably have very little contact with him or her. Real estate professionals have learned from hard experience that it is not wise for buyers and sellers to have too much contact before the transaction closes. You will notice that if they are present at all, they typically keep a very low profile during home showings.

There are, however, several important obligations that a seller has to the buyer. One of the most significant is the requirement to disclose material facts. If the roof leaks, that's a material fact and should be disclosed. Many states now have mandatory disclosure laws, and we will discuss the subject in detail later in Chapter 12, but it's a valuable concept to emphasize and for you to keep in mind.

There also is a real estate fact of life you need to remember. The overwhelming majority of lawsuits in real estate transactions are brought by unhappy buyers, not sellers. The sellers have typically collected their huge check and are often long gone from the area (perhaps the country) and will not be available for redress if something goes awry. It is best, therefore, to get everything tied up in writing as neatly as possible when everyone is present and accounted for. Thus, obtaining a forwarding address is a good idea, as well as employment information.

For Sale by Owner (FSBO)

To real estate agents, these are known as Fizzbos. The primary motivation in selling homes without an agent is to save the commission that would have to be paid to a broker.

There are several cautions you must observe in dealing with the Fizzbo. First, the house is often overpriced. In a hot sellers' market in particular, homeowners frequently get an inflated view of what their homes are worth. Your job will be to become very informed on property values. You do this by looking at a lot of properties and investigating official assessed values, typically available as a public record in county or city offices. If you are working with a real estate agent in looking at other homes, you can get some good on-the-job education regarding home values by asking a lot of questions. Of course, if it turns out that the home has been underpriced (rare, but possible), you may have uncovered a gem.

Finally, in working with Fizzbos you need to rely even more on your attorney and other professionals such as inspectors and escrow and title agents. Become very familiar with the entire homebuying process, for there will be no friendly real estate professionals whose payday depends upon satisfying everyone, including you, to get the transaction closed.

Lenders

I'm sure you've heard of the golden rule as it relates to mortgage lending—those who have the gold make the rules. That is basically true. You want their money, you play by their rules; so you have to learn the rules. The basic rule is that lenders stay profitable by making loans to people who pay them back. That means they will take a very hard look at you and the house you want to buy, and they've had a lot of experience evaluating people and property. Some have said that the surefire way of getting a mortgage loan is to prove that you absolutely don't need the money. Although there is some truth to this, it would be more accurate to say that what you have to prove is that you will absolutely pay the money back.

Inspectors

We will deal with the topic of inspection in some detail in Chapter 12, but it is valuable to mention inspectors in this context. You should know who the inspector is working for and why the inspection was done. If a seller, for example, has an inspection done in conjunction with listing the home, it is just possible that the inspector knows not to be too picky when checking things out. As we will emphasize in Chapter 12, the best arrangement is to hire your own inspector.

Escrow and Title Companies

These parties will be involved after the offer to purchase has been accepted and the closing process begins. A variety of activities will occur, such as researching the title, checking the public records for liens, working with lenders, figuring out who owes how much to whom, preparing deeds, collecting funds and disbursing them and recording appropriate documents in the public records.

Practices vary widely around the country as to who performs the actual closing (when documents and money change hands) and the activities that precede and follow it. In many places escrow and title companies are involved. *Escrow* is a process in which money and documents are held by a disinterested third party until all the terms of the transaction have satisfactorily been satisfied. Remember our discussion of agency as it related to real estate agents. Escrow companies are disclosed dual agents. In other words, they represent both the buyer and the seller, with the written consent of each. That means until the buyer and seller agree on a matter, the process stops.

Costs of escrow are typically shared by the buyer and seller. Title companies are often associated with escrow companies. They research the title and they issue title insurance. We'll cover that in more detail in Chapter 15.

Picking a Product

After all the preliminaries are out of the way, you are finally ready to step into the marketplace and select the home of your choice. Well, maybe not quite yet. First you must think about what type of home you want. We'll now consider the advantages and disadvantages of your major options.

● ● ▼ ●

Red Flag Checklist and Survival Strategies

1. A real estate agent advises you not to waste your money hiring an attorney.

Strategy: If the advice is given while in a moving vehicle, wait for it to stop. Then get out and get another agent.

2. The blood seems to drain from the face of a homeseller when you ask about the roof and the subject gets changed very quickly after an evasive answer.

Strategy: Be a very attentive and perceptive question asker. Ask the tough questions, gauge the reaction and follow up. In a situation such as this, an even more thorough inspection than normal may be warranted.

3.   In checking with an escrow company on the type of services they offer, you are assured that they can provide guidance on such matters as the best method of taking title.

Strategy: This qualifies as legal advice and is not within the purview of normal escrow activities. If the escrow company had a legal department and the advice came from there, that would be another matter. Escrow agents may infrequently slip over the line and offer legal advice, as can real estate licensees.

4.   The leading real estate broker in town also owns an insurance company and an escrow and title company, which are all located in the same building.

Strategy: I personally favor having these functions performed by completely independent offices. Even though any connection will probably have to be disclosed to you and it is convenient, I still much prefer an arrangement where all tasks are performed by wholly autonomous entities.

5.   A company in a large metropolitan area advertises immediate mortgage loan approvals by phone.

Strategy: A lender can determine very quickly whether or not you will qualify, assuming what you are telling them is true. Any such approval will have to be contingent upon the verification of all information. Call me old-fashioned if you will, but I still prefer to borrow (or lend) money in eyeball-to-eyeball meetings.

6.   An attorney with whom you confer informs you that she believes you are planning to pay way too much for the home you have in mind.

Strategy: I would certainly respect that opinion and would reevaluate my plans. However, that's not typically why you retain an attorney, and rarely would an attorney offer that kind of an opinion. Their expertise is law, not real estate values.

7.   A homeowner who is selling his own home informs you that it has already been inspected and that another inspection is not necessary.

Strategy: Except in very unusual circumstances, insist upon a current inspection as a contingency, even if you have to pay for it. Sellers who use phrases like "an inspection won't be necessary" worry me.

8. In looking at a Fizzbo, you are informed that several homes in the immediate area have sold recently for an amount in excess of asking price.

Strategy: Information like this is often based upon hearsay or wishful thinking. Sellers frequently inflate actual figures to impress their neighbors. In working with Fizzbos, you have an added incentive to check official records to verify all information you're given.

9. You are informed by the owner of a home that he will give you a quitclaim deed.

Strategy: This is the deed with the least amount of protection for the buyer. Insist that your attorney approve any deed you are offered. You will likely be counseled to insist upon a warranty deed or to look elsewhere.

10. A homeowner in a neighborhood you are considering volunteers the information that the CC&Rs in that development are quite restrictive. It's the first time you've heard of a CC&R.

Strategy: CC&R stands for conditions, covenants and restrictions. They will be a matter of public record, and before you make any offer to purchase you need to carefully review them. There could be restrictions on such mundane things as what color you may paint your house. CC&Rs generally enhance value, but they can be very restrictive, so you will want to read them thoroughly.

5

......▼......

Which Castle Is Right for You?

I don't wish to anger you, but there is a saying in the real estate business that goes "buyers are liars." The reason for that goes something like this: "The Dumpsters told me they absolutely must have a four-bedroom, three-bath home in the suburbs. For weeks that's what I showed them. They ended up buying a two-bedroom condo in a downtown high-rise from a competitor. Go figure."

Are Purchasers Prevaricators?

Experiences like that are frustrating if you are a real estate professional working with homebuyers, but there are some rational explanations. There are also some irrational explanations. We'll take the rational first.

● ●

Not in My Backyard!

In most instances buyers do know what they want, or at least they think they do, and typically end up purchasing pretty much what they said they had in mind. But not always. For example, in our move to our present home we made a commitment to our horse-loving daughter that we would buy a home with enough acreage for her to have a horse. (In retrospect, that ranks right up there with one of the dumbest promises we ever made, but that's another story.) What we ended up buying was a home with enough acreage for a horse but with zoning that prohibited horses. However, just down the hill, out of sight and out of smell, was a horse-boarding setup that satisfied our young equestrian and delighted us. We were not lying. We thought we knew what we wanted. It just turned out that there was a creative solution to our problem that was even better.

● ●

Horse-Sense Solutions

As you are mapping out your homebuying campaign, you need to consider all the alternatives available to you and establish some criteria to guide your search. What are the most important features to you? On what will you compromise? What's the top dollar you will, or can, pay? Share this information with the real estate professional who is assisting you. Make it clear that although you are flexible and willing to at least listen to innovative proposals (you should be—remember the horse story), you've thought about this carefully and have mapped your general strategy. Otherwise, you may end up looking at a lot of homes that aren't even remote possibilities for you.

You should also be firm with the agent and clearly establish that you are in charge of the situation. Regrettably, there are instances where homebuyers irrationally alter their course and end up buying what a smooth-talking real estate agent wanted to sell them rather than what they really wanted to buy. It's possible that the Dumpsters ran into one of them. More on these things later, but to help you reach those initial decisions, be aware of the major options open to you and the most important advantages and disadvantages of each option. You will have a lot of choices. We'll look further at the basic menu in this chapter.

Single-Family Detached

The single-family detached home accounts for roughly three-quarters of all home sales in the United States. It's what most people think about first when they consider buying a home.

This type of home is the embodiment of the American Dream. For many people, it's their own hunk of land. Within the context of governmental zoning laws, private residential restrictions imposed by deeds and a variety of other restraints (such as peer pressure from stern neighbors), people can do absolutely anything they want with a single-family detached home. These homes come in two basic varieties: (1) old (preowned) and (2) new.

Preowned

Most of the available homes are preowned. They typically account for about 90 percent of all single-family detached home sales, depending on the strength of the new home market in any particular year. It is difficult to generalize about advantages and disadvantages of a preowned home (or "preloved," as one creative ad writer put it), since this category can include everything from a 4,000-square-foot, ultramodern, six-month-old home that the original owners had to sell unexpectedly to a century-old Victorian to a 1,200-square-foot, post–World War II, cookie-cutter ranch. Nonetheless, here are some thoughts on the pluses and minuses of the preowned home.

The Balance Sheet

- *Price.* Preowned homes typically cost less than the same sized new home, so you'll get more house for your money. Whether you get a better house for your money depends upon the individual circumstances. It will help you understand the valuation process better, if you know how the prices of new homes are determined, since they set the market value of preowned homes.

  The pricing of preowned homes is not a precise science. Neither is the pricing of new homes, but it comes a lot closer. If it's a spec house (built on the speculation that the builder will locate a buyer), the new home builder will get a commitment for financing at a local bank, buy a lot, order building materials, do the construction (which includes hiring a lot of subcontractors) and then arrange for marketing. All of this costs money, much of it "on the cuff." The builder totals up costs and adds a profit margin. In a competitive environment there's usually not much of a margin; and since the builder will probably need to sell the house before the construction loan can be paid off, the meter is running. There is, therefore, a great incentive to price a spec home right and move it quickly. The one element that's absent in this equation is appreciation.

Let's say that ten years down the road the purchaser of that spec home puts it on the market. There's been a decade of appreciation as well as alterations and additions. There's a yard with a sprinkler system. Children have been born and their growth patterns marked lovingly on the kitchen wall. There's a lot of sentimental attachment. The owner hears that neighbors down the street got $20,000 more than they actually did when they sold their house (which clearly wasn't even in the same league with theirs). Pricing tends to get extremely subjective. The bottom line is this: Establish a standard of comparison by pricing out new homes. Then look at a lot of preowned homes in your general price range. You will then have a better handle on true market value.

- *Location.* If a neighborhood is established, you know what it will be like when it "grows up." You can see if there is a pride of ownership among the neighbors. You can evaluate the availability and quality of such things as schools, public transportation, fire protection, shopping, medical facilities and recreational opportunities.

  New homes are typically built on the fringes of the growth boundaries, and many of these services may still be in the planning stages. There are, of course, some new home developments that take place on spectacular hunks of ground and are developed with wide streets, underground utilities and numerous natural areas.

- *Lot Size.* One of the biggest factors in the cost of building a new home is the price of land. As Will Rogers so aptly observed, "They ain't making any more of it." The end result is that developers are apt to try to get as many houses as possible on a tract of land. With resales, you will often find a very modest older home on a very generous plot of ground. That could be a plus for you or a minus, depending upon how thrilled you are with tending to a large yard. From a value standpoint, it's definitely a plus.

- *Variety.* Your selection will be nearly limitless—from cute Cape Cods to elegant English Tudors as well as a great variety of other less impressive (and expensive) options. While there is certainly variety in new home construction, it's really not possible to match the array of distinctive architectural styles that characterizes the preowned market.

- *Construction.* There is a perception that "they don't build 'em the way they use to." To that, some folks answer, "Thank God." It's true that hardwood floors were once the norm and now it's carpeting over plywood. It's also true that there are, in fact, some extremely well-built older homes that are quite likely to outlast us all. On the other hand, it is equally true that the older the home, the more wary you have to be for such problems as asbestos, lead paint, leaky pipes, inadequate insulation, electrical systems that provide unanticipated displays of fireworks and bugs that eat wood.

- *Financing.* Lending institutions have the most experience in making loans on preowned homes, so they are very comfortable with the system. They are also very well versed in how to spot potential problems with the property and with the borrower, and they know what steps are needed to eliminate or reduce risks. Lending institutions will insist on such things as inspections, independent appraisals and title insurance, which all work to your advantage, even though the process may seem tedious at times.

- *Upkeep.* The discouraging fact about both buildings and human bodies is that they wear out—on a fairly predictable schedule. A building-inspector friend of mine, who appears occasionally at my real estate class, suggests that at about the 15-year point, houses really start to show the stress of age. The good news is that buildings can be repaired; the bad news is the price. It's expensive. Trust me. Our house is 18 years old. If you are considering a home that is "teenager" (or older), pay extremely close attention when we discuss inspections.

- *Warranties.* There's been a trend to offer limited home warranties with resale homes. If the seller has paid for a limited home warranty, it is a plus, but hard experience with them shows that there often are major exceptions, high deductibles and substantial fees for each service call. Study the fine print and know the time limits of the coverage. Do not assume that because a warranty is offered there is less necessity for impartial inspections. As a matter of fact, some sellers may conclude that if they offer a warranty, they are relieved of making full disclosure of problems.

- *Handyperson Specials.* These certainly qualify as preowned homes, but they deserve to be in a category all their own. For some people it's a romantic fantasy to find an old clunker of a house, buy it at a bargain price, tenderly and lovingly restore it, live in it happily for a few years and then sell it for a huge profit. Some call it the "This Old House" syndrome. If you are or become afflicted, proceed with particular caution. Here's why.

   First, you must know enough about houses to recognize a genuine diamond in the rough when you see one. Second, you must be able to accurately judge what it will take in terms of dollars to do the job without bankrupting you. Third, unless you have successful experience in renovating old houses, you will find it extremely difficult to secure financing. Lending institutions tend to consider these projects high-risk with more potential aggravation than they're worth. If you haven't had appropriate experience, you'll probably have to look outside the mainstream for your money, which generally means friends, relatives (the Mom and Dad S&L) or lenders you meet on street corners late at night and who charge exorbitant interest.

• •

Eureka!

For those hopeless romantics among you, here's a bit of encouragement. I once worked with a young couple who told me they wanted a fixer-upper. I had trouble with that since I knew what was available locally in that category and I could never imagine myself buying a house where you could stick your finger through the exterior wall. I also knew they could qualify for a lot more home than they said they wanted. (Be prepared for a lot of skepticism and looks of incredulity if you tell a real estate agent you want to buy less house than you can afford. We rarely encounter that.) After several unsuccessful showings of homes in which I thought they would be happier (yes, they were somewhat more expensive), I sensed I was about to lose them so I broke down and showed them a real dump. I vividly recall the husband walking up to an outside wall and reaching for a long strand of ivy growing up the side. As he pulled it away, half the wall came with it. You would have thought he had just won Lotto America. The couple became even more ecstatic when they found that the dining room floor was uneven, the roof leaked and the garage looked as though it couldn't survive a strong sneeze. They bought the home, carefully restored it, lived in it for several years and sold it at an astounding profit. Besides working with an exceptionally astute real estate agent, they did have several things going for them, including quite a good supply of cash, good jobs, a whole lot of determination and a willingness to get their hands dirty. It can be done, but keep the stars out of your eyes and your feet firmly planted on the ground.

● ●

New Homes

There is a special thrill about shopping for, buying and living in a new home. Everyone should do it at least once. If you don't do it right, however, once may be enough.

The Balance Sheet

- *Modern Design.* One of the exciting things about a new home is that everything is in fact brand-new. The furnace is energy-efficient. The double-pane windows ensure that the curtains don't stand straight out when the wind blows hard. The hot-water heater does its job without sounding like the Chattanooga Choo Choo going up Mt. Everest. The oven is spotless, permitting you to be the first to spill peach cobbler in it. There is no shag carpeting, and none of the appliances are colored harvest gold. The thrill of driving home in a new car and turning the heads of envious neighbors pales in comparison. It really is a truly memorable experience.

- *Operations and Maintenance.* Those who tout the benefits of new homes point to the fact that they are less expensive to operate and maintain. In most cases that is true. If you buy a home built before 1980, it will probably not be energy-efficient unless it has been upgraded. Since your single largest operations outlay will be for utilities, the difference can amount to a few hundred dollars per month or more. Property insurance will probably also be cheaper. If, for example, you live in a house with a 20-year-old wood shake roof, that factor alone will cost you extra insurance dollars.

New homes will obviously require less corrective maintenance, barring any construction shortcomings. There are those who say (typically, those who build or sell new houses) that your savings in operations, maintenance and insurance alone will allow you to buy a more expensive new home and still pay about the same in monthly housing costs. You need to pencil that out for yourself, since it will depend upon your exact local circumstances and the specific homes you are considering.

- *Warranties.* New homes ordinarily come with formal home warranties. Even if they don't, there is an implied habitability to which builders are held by most states and local jurisdictions. That simply means that if you buy a new home and something goes wrong within a year or so (length of time varies), the builder will be responsible for correcting it. Formal warranty plans differ in coverage. The Home Owner's Warranty (HOW) is the most well known. It's a ten-year extended warranty for which member builders pay a one-time premium when the house is built. It covers workmanship and material for one year, major systems such as electrical and plumbing for two years and the structure of the house for ten years.

  Consumers sometimes rely too heavily on new home warranties. There are exclusions to coverage and time limits within which claims must be filed. If you buy a home with a warranty, read the warranty right away and very carefully. Become familiar with the claims procedure and file quickly if one is needed. Far more important than any warranty program is the willingness and ability of your builder to respond to your concerns. The vast majority of consumer complaints are resolved directly with builders without formally resorting to the provisions of any warranty. High on the list of desired qualities is a long track record of successful operations and satisfied customers in the local area. Membership in professional organizations, such as the National Association of Home Builders, is also a plus.

- *Appreciation.* For the first few years, new homes typically appreciate at a faster pace than comparable resale properties. In some extremely hot markets appreciation can be astonishing. In some insanely hot markets purchasers have been known to camp out for days to be the first in line to complete an offer to purchase. That sounds idiotic until you understand that in these cases new homes appreciate up to 20 to 30 thousand dollars in a few months. Some people sell their contracts without ever moving in. Be advised that this is not the norm and will appeal mainly to those of you who have no qualms about investing your hard-earned money in such things as pork belly futures.

- *Financing.* While new homes typically cost more per square foot than older homes, financing is often very conveniently packaged. That's assuming you qualify, of course. Builders understand that they must have financing lined up to market their product and that they must be competitive. There will have been a financial institution involved in the construction financing, so there aren't apt to be any problems with such things as appraisals. Many lenders will already have arranged what is known as *takeout financing,* in which permanent consumer loans that will replace the construction loans have already been set up. It will simply remain for the buyer to pick an option and to qualify.

Custom Homes.   When most people buy a new home, they purchase one that is being built or is already finished. In large developments, model homes are constructed, furnished and landscaped. You tour these developments and look over the construction going on, or about to start, in the project. Prices have been fixed, and the remaining options open to the purchaser depend on how far along the construction is.

With a custom building job, a buyer locates a building lot and a builder to construct a home to the buyer's plans and specifications. Assuming they agree on price and financing is obtained, the house gets built and everyone is happy. The advantage of this arrangement is that the buyer gets exactly the home they want, or at least what they can afford.

There are major cautions. These jobs almost always seem to cost more and take longer than anyone had anticipated. There must be a real rapport between buyer and builder, and the lines of communication have to be kept open. If you're married, take special note. Marriage counselors and divorce lawyers whom I respect tell me the only thing that will test a marital relationship more is a major remodelling job in an existing home.

Your Other Options

Whether new or old, the single-family home is the choice of the great majority of homebuyers. But whether by necessity or preference, many look for other options. There are actually some pretty good ones.

• •▼• •

Red Flag Checklist and Survival Strategies

1. You see an ad for a fixer-upper in the local paper. It includes the phrase "needs work."

Strategy: Don't be such a skeptic. You can believe the ad. It will truly need work—lots of work. The question is, "Can you do the work (or get it done) at a price that will make it a better deal than buying one that doesn't need work?"

2. In touring model homes in a new subdivision you marvel at all the beautiful drapes, carpeting and incredibly beautiful furniture.

Strategy: Be very sure you know what is included in the price and what is not. Model homes typically will feature the latest in fashionable furniture. That's obviously not included. They may also be outfitted with optional (as in extra price) items such as intercom systems, garage door openers, microwaves, saunas, hot tubs and vacuum systems. Everything that is not included should be clearly marked but isn't always.

3. The builder of the new home for which you want to make an offer to purchase is known as No Dicker Danielle.

Strategy: Prices on new homes are usually fairly firm, but that depends upon the market and the individual circumstance. Even if Danielle won't dicker on the price, she may throw in a few goodies such as a drape allowance or a security alarm system. Don't be intimidated. Make a proposal. Danielle won't be mad at you. Put it in writing.

4. You've found a great little fixer-upper but are somewhat concerned about the run-down condition of the surrounding houses.

Strategy: Look very, very carefully at the neighborhood. If your house is the only beautiful swan in a sea of ugly ducklings, it will be judged by the company it keeps.

5. A real estate agent with whom you are working informs you that one particular listing that sounds interesting to you is being offered "as is."

Strategy: Not only should this wave a red flag in front of you, it should cause alarm bells to ring. Some property owners think offering a home "as is" gives them a license to fib, conceal, obfuscate and keep mum on material defects. It doesn't, but you should find out clearly what specifically prompted the "as is" clause.

6. In looking at a home on an established city lot, it appears as though the side of the house is almost on the property line. The owner maintains that there is a variance that permits this encroachment.

Strategy: *Variance* is the right word. This means that formal permission by the appropriate governmental agency has been given to permit deviation from a zoning law—in this case, a setback requirement from the property line. Verify that there is in fact a recorded variance. On rare occasions, property owners have been required to alter or demolish buildings that encroach without permission.

7. You own a recreation vehicle approximately one block long and are looking for a home with a long enough driveway in which to park it.

Strategy: Be very sure that the home you decide upon is not in a development with restrictions against parking recreation vehicles so that they may be seen from the street. Many do, particularly new developments.

8. You are considering a home with a great view of the city, which would be even greater if you cut a few trees on your property.

Strategy: Check out local ordinances and deed restrictions. Some places have rules against cutting any mature trees without permission, whether on your property or not.

9. *When you ask the owner of a property what the official assessed value is, the subject quickly gets changed.*

Strategy: Chances are the asking price far exceeds the official assessed value. Check with the city or county assessor's office. It's public information. It isn't unusual for market value to exceed tax assessment value, and methods of assessment vary from state to state; but if there is a big difference, do further comparative shopping.

10. *The home you are considering is the largest, most expensive in the neighborhood.*

Strategy: Okay, this is an easy one. From a value standpoint what you want is the least expensive home in a very nice neighborhood. But if the big house is the one your head and your heart say you want and it seems to be priced right compared to similar properties, go for it.

6

·····▼·····

Different Folks, Different Strokes: Condos and Co-ops

Even if you have decided that your unswerving goal is to buy the traditional single-family home in the suburbs, you may alter your views based on financial realities or on learning of other possibilities you had not fully considered. So whether you're motivated by economic necessity or simply by a desire to be completely informed before making a major decision, be aware of your other options. Condos and co-ops are popular choices for many people.

Condominiums

Condominium (or *condo*) ownership is basically a simple concept. You own your individual living unit in a building with other units.

Here's an example. You are renting a two-bedroom, two-bath apartment in the Palace Towers, a 100-unit luxury apartment complex. You pay your monthly rent and have certain rights. The owners decide to convert the Towers to condominiums. You like the idea, so you buy your unit. You are now the owner of that apartment.

What you actually own is an identifiable cube of air in the building. In many ways condo ownership is the same as ownership of a single-family detached home. There are differences (which we will discuss later in this chapter), but if you own a condo, it's a statutory entity. You will get an individual deed when you buy a condo. You can then sell it, lease it out, borrow money on it or give it away (call me). It will be treated by your friendly property tax authorities in the same manner as a single-family detached house. If your neighbor down the hall fails to make a mortgage payment and the bank forecloses, it has no impact on you.

In a condo you also have an ownership interest in the common areas of the complex, such as the land, parking facilities, stairways, swimming pool, exterior structure and so on. This is called an undivided common interest because your right to use the facilities is not dependent on the size or cost of your unit, although how much say you have in how the complex is run may be.

The Balance Sheet

Price.   Some people love the idea of condo ownership, and others hate it. Some who are not all that thrilled with the idea may opt for it for one simple reason—in many places it's a lot cheaper than a single-family detached home. This will be a difficult fact for you to accept if the only condos you are familiar with are developments with names like Country Club Haven and Rockerfeller Manor and have Jags and BMWs parked in front of them. Statistically, however, it's true. In some markets the average sales price of a condo will be 40 to 50 percent less than the single-family detached option.

Variety.   Remember that the word *condominium* describes a form of ownership, not a type of building. Although the apartment-style condo is common, there are an infinite variety. They range from a very modest apartment building that has been converted to lavish single-level units built specifically as condos and clustered around a golf course.

Quality of Construction.   Several years ago, as the condo concept became more accepted by homebuyers, a conversion feeding frenzy occurred. Let's say you owned an apartment building that with intensive management was barely returning a positive cash flow for you. An astute developer shows you how to convert the apartments to condos and sell them. The profit figures he projects take your breath away. You're convinced and you convert. So did a lot of other apartment house owners.

Consumer abuses occurred during this period, prompting many state legislatures to enact very restrictive rules on condo conversions. One of the biggest complaints had to do with quality of construction. "Paper-thin walls" was a complaint often heard. A tenant who pays $700 a month for an apartment might be slightly annoyed by the presence of a noisy neighbor. A purchaser who pays $100,000 for that apartment as a condo would likely be more than somewhat irritated by that same inconsiderate neighbor.

New construction, built specifically as condos, naturally gets much better marks. For example, when we moved to our present location, a local builder was just in the early stages of constructing a condominium project. We purchased a condo for a relative when it was in the foundation stage. Each individual unit had its own interior walls, separated by an airspace as opposed to a common wall. It was clear in all the planning and actual construction that these units were designed as homes, not as apartments. Since it was early in the construction process, my wife and mother-in-law could work with the builder to customize the condo. It turned out well for us, and the builder maintains that the nervous twitch he developed had nothing to do with the experience.

Condominium Owners' Association.   This is an association of elected condo owners who control and manage the overall affairs of the condo complex, including maintenance of the common areas, such as the required periodic painting of the exterior as well as such exotic functions as garbage pickup. Those things obviously cost money, and they seem to cost more money each year. You will be required to pay monthly dues to cover these expenses. By the way, if you buy a condo, the amount of these fees will be considered by a lender when qualifying you for the loan. Condo associations have some rather formidable power. For example, miss some of those dues payments and they can put a lien on your property—and in a worst-case situation, actually foreclose on it.

• •

Monarch or Serf?

In condo living you give up a lot of your royal powers. You are no longer the more or less absolute ruler of your own domain. For example, let's say you wished to decorate the outside of your condo door with large paintings of your favorite flowers. Or perhaps you want to plant a giant redwood next to your parking stall. Or maybe you envision getting a waiver to condo rules that prohibit pets to realize your lifelong desire to have a pair of Dobermans and train them to attack on command. As reasonable as all of these proposals may appear, there's probably not much chance of getting the association to okay any of them. On balance this will work to your financial advantage, for as impeccable as your judgment may be in matters such as these, there's no accounting for the tastes of others, and maintaining a standard of conformity will enhance property values.

• •

Convenience.   In a condo you can quit worrying about maintaining the outside of your home. No more hustling to find a painter who will start the job on time and finish before the monsoon season hits. For those who have become a bit weary of watering, weeding and mowing, the luxury of having someone else do that for you is quite appealing. And there's no need to line up anyone to look out after the place when you go on vacation or a long business trip. For example, an acquaintance of mine is a retired professor from the local university. He and his wife purchased a condo recently, and the last time I talked to them they were planning an extended trip to Germany. Their grass will be just as green and weed-free when they return as it was when they left.

Security.   There are some really upscale condo developments where security, including 24-hour guards and controlled access, is a top priority. It's an unfortunate fact of contemporary life that in many areas this feature alone makes condo living a very attractive alternative. In addition to providing a secure environment, there are some projects that have incorporated housekeeping support, transportation services, recreational opportunities (golf courses are popular), health care and nursing facilities into their developments.

Insurance.   A final caution on condos. Your condominium owners' association will carry liability insurance for the common areas. There have been cases where that liability insurance has been inadequate to cover an unexpectedly large claim, and individual condo owners have become vulnerable to make up the difference. It is good to check this out with your attorney and your insurance company to make sure your individual liability coverage is adequate or that association bylaws protect you.

Cooperatives

Unless you live in New York, Chicago or a handful of other areas, you probably have never heard of co-ops. It is not a concept that has taken America by storm. The owner of a co-op apartment doesn't actually own real estate but is a shareholder in a corporation whose principal asset is a building. In return for that stock, the shareholder is given a proprietary lease that grants occupancy in an apartment. Each proprietary lease owner pays a share of the corporation's expenses, which include the overall mortgage, property taxes and maintenance. If the lease is properly structured, the shareholder can deduct taxes and interest for income tax purposes. Sounds complicated, doesn't it? It is, but at least it does permit a form of ownership. It also provides a few additional headaches that are unique.

The Balance Sheet

Assignability.   This is a fancy word that means you can sell your interests in a contract without restriction. The problem with co-ops is that ordinarily you cannot do this. If you want to sell your co-op apartment, you typically need to have the permission of the co-op's board of directors. If you want to sell to someone whom the board thinks might not fit in, you can be prevented from doing so. By law, discrimination based upon such things as race, gender, creed, sex, familial status, handicap or national origin are not permitted, but there are untold other attributes co-op boards can object to. Many boards even prohibit subletting your apartment.

Joint Responsibility.   As you will recall, in the condo arrangement if your neighbor misses a mortgage payment, it is of no consequence to you. If your co-op neighbor misses payments, it is, because the corporation takes out a single mortgage and makes payments using funds provided by the monthly payments of shareholders. Missed payments by individuals must be made up for by other shareholders, or the corporate mortgage can be in danger of default.

Price.   This is the major reason co-ops exist. Let me give you a specific, dramatic example. A recent issue of the *Westchester* (N.Y.) *Realtor* carried comparative sales figures in Westchester County for the previous three years. Are you ready for this? The latest average sales price of a single-family home was $353,396. Before you get discouraged and decide to give up your homebuying plans, I should point out that Westchester County is one of the most expensive housing markets in the country. Except for a few other ritzy areas, homes will almost certainly cost less where you live. (By the way, if you decide all this is so fascinating you want to give up your practice as a brain surgeon and sell real estate for a living, move to Westchester County. Six percent of $353,396! Mercy.)

Back to the price of co-ops. In the same period I mentioned for Westchester County, co-ops accounted for about 10 percent of total sales, and the average sales price was $88,160, or roughly 25 percent that of a single-family home! So it is fairly clear that the thought process for many co-op buyers is "it's either this or nothing."

● ●

This Is a Good Deal?

I must admit that I've had no firsthand experience with co-ops. I actually know only one person who owns a co-op. She is an editor for a major publishing company who lives in New York. I met her first at a conference in Chicago in 1987. At that point she was just in the process of buying into a co-op. She paid $133,000 for a 700-square-foot apartment, or a tidy $190 per square foot, just slightly less than what Buckingham Palace would go for. The next time I saw her was in 1993 at another conference in Chicago. In the interim the value of her apartment (her stock) had decreased to the point where it was worth less than the amount she owed on it, making it impossible to refinance her higher-than-market-rate loan. If she had to sell, she would have to eat over $35,000, which represented her down payment. She couldn't lease it out, since it is 100 percent owner occupied with no rentals allowed.

● ●

While declining market value is not a situation peculiar to co-ops, they seem particularly vulnerable during down markets. For example, take a look at the Westchester County situation I mentioned. Note that while the sales price of single-family homes and condos increased slightly, co-ops fell by over 8 percent and it took longer to sell them. Although my editor friend (who, by the way, lives in Westchester County) is clearly not a big booster of co-ops from an investment standpoint, she is satisfied that it was the only realistic homeowning option she had and that living there has satisfied an even more important objective: providing a good school district for her son.

Westchester County, N.Y.

	1991	1992	1993
Single-Family Homes			
Avg. sales price	$351,273	$356,131	$353,396
Avg. days on market	203	192	192
Condominiums			
Avg. sales price	$170,568	$171,782	$174,243
Avg. days on market	186	202	208
Cooperatives			
Avg. sales price	$96,740	$90,799	$88,160
Avg. days on market	207	223	256

Source: *Westchester Realtor.*

Red Flag Checklist
and Survival Strategies

1. You've never really thought living in a commune would be much fun.

Strategy: Short of moving to Berkeley, living in a co-op probably comes the closest to communal living. Read all documents very carefully, including the bylaws and the proprietary lease, to make certain you can live with them.

Remember that other people will be making important lifestyle and financial decisions for you, including who can buy you out.

2. A local apartment house has been converted into a condominium project and is advertising units that are about $10,000 cheaper than other local condos with comparable square footage.

Strategy: It is quite possible that the quality of construction in a conversion condo will be more than adequate. On the other hand, it may feature thin walls, skimpy insulation, horrible floor plans and outdated appliances. If the condo is a conversion, probe thoroughly and ponder carefully.

3. When considering a condo as a possible purchase, you notice several For Rent signs on other units.

Strategy: You need to find out exactly what percentage of occupants in the condo complex are renters. The higher the proportion of owner-occupants, the better; they tend to take a more personal interest in their property and how things are run. Some lenders won't loan money on a condo if there is an unusually high percentage of renters. Some have even established specific criteria such as 90 percent owner-occupants mandatory.

4. You are a senior citizen and find what looks like a great deal on a condo. The price is way below market and financing is convenient. The only unusual provision is that you must agree to deed the property to the developer upon your demise.

Strategy: I won't insult your intelligence by suggesting that you first look up *demise* in your Funk & Wagnall's. There are some very reputable charitable and religious organizations with somewhat similar programs that appear to work to everyone's satisfaction. On the other hand, I'm not at all sure that I would be comfortable in a situation wherein my death would prove to be a major benefit to someone outside my immediate family. Check with your attorney and relatives you trust.

5. In touring a condo complex you walk across a wooden bridge in the central courtyard that looks as though it's about to collapse.

Strategy: This is a very bad sign on two counts. First, the property isn't being properly maintained. Second, if someone falls through the rickety bridge and is injured seriously, you could be looking at a big lawsuit against the association.

6. You have purchased a co-op apartment and find that the built-in stove doesn't function properly.

Strategy: Your recourse is from the person who sold you the co-op interest, not the co-op board of directors. It's not like an apartment complex, where you call the super.

7. Your mother's eyesight is impaired to the extent that she must use a Seeing Eye dog, but the condo complex in which she wishes to buy has a no-pet rule.

Strategy: Federal law mandates that a person be permitted to have a Seeing Eye dog in such a situation. If the condo authorities don't know that, have your attorney give them a buzz.

8. You are a senior citizen who would really prefer a condo complex where there are no children permitted, but your real estate agent tells you that's not allowed anymore.

Strategy: Wrong. Assuming the development follows certain specific rules (for example all units occupied by persons 62 years of age or older), it is perfectly legal.

9. In touring a condo development you see absolutely no empty parking places anywhere.

Strategy: You've put your finger on one of the biggest annoyances of many condo complexes that were converted from apartments. You may have only one space allocated to your unit, and if someone else parks in that space, you will have to hike. Newer developments typically plan better.

10. Your wife is pregnant with your second child. The real estate agent tells you that the two-bedroom condo you are looking at is not appropriate since there is an association rule that limits the two-bedroom units to three people.

Strategy: This would likely be viewed as a case of discrimination based upon familial status and therefore not legal. Two people per bedroom is considered appropriate, depending on the size of the rooms, of course. Run it by your attorney.

7

·····▼·····

More Folks, More Strokes

Just in case we haven't yet pushed your hot button with our discussion of housing options, let's consider a few others. We will start with what is a real fascination for many—rural property.

Country Property

If you decide to slip on the jeans, lace up the boots and move to the boonies, you need answers to a number of questions before you commit yourself to five acres and independence in the country. In this discussion we are talking about country property that you would buy primarily as a home. If you decide to purchase a 200-acre ranch for your herd of Texas longhorns, that's another subject.

Can You Identify It?

If you buy a standard lot in a new subdivision in the city, the chances are pretty good that the boundaries will be well marked and identifiable. However, if you buy an irregularly shaped parcel in the country, things may be a little less well defined. Here's a quick example.

• •

You Mean All This Is Ours?

We live on a 1.83-acre parcel in the country. When we bought the home, our eager-to-please real estate agent did a quick paceoff of the property lines to let us know what we were buying. He referred to the information contained in the multiple listing, using some trees that had been planted at the edge of the property as a starting point. He kept walking and walking. It looked good to us. About six months after we moved in, we decided to get a formal survey. We got quite a surprise. Except for the fact that the previous owners had planted two small Douglas fir trees in our uphill neighbor's yard (I later moved them to our property), our lot was a great deal more desirable than we had originally thought. We had an expansive side yard that we believed belonged to our downhill neighbors. Now, what if the news had not been good? What if we had received a much worse lot than we thought we had bargained for? You know—litigation city. It's much better to avoid that whole scene.

• •

No matter what assurances you are given, never buy a piece of country property that hasn't been recently surveyed and the property lines clearly marked. Surveys cost money, so sellers may be reluctant to comply; but however you work it out, do it. Don't compromise on this issue. Sign nothing you cannot get out of until you know exactly what you're getting.

Can You Build on It?

Driving down a beautiful rural road, you come upon what looks to you like a perfect spot to build your dream home. It has a For Sale sign on it. It may, in fact, be an ideal building site. On the other hand, it may have restrictive zoning that prohibits or severely limits building. For example, I once encountered a small acreage parcel next to property with a mature stand of fir trees. It looked like a great place to build, but because the trees were periodically sprayed, there could be no building within a certain setback, which eliminated the most desirable building site.

The property may even have an older home on it that is there now as a nonconforming use. That means it was originally in conformance with zoning laws, but the laws have changed and the home is permitted to stay as an exception to them. It probably means you couldn't tear the home down and build another one or even add on to the current home. It may also mean that if it burned down, you wouldn't be able to rebuild. It also could mean that you couldn't build an additional residential structure even if there were plenty of acreage to accommodate the structure. Whether it's bare land or country property with buildings on it, check out the zoning thoroughly.

How's the Water?

There are two critical elements involved here: (1) quantity and (2) quality. Quantity can be estimated informally by simply turning on a few taps at the same time to see what happens to the volume of the water. Formally, it is gauged by a water flow test to determine gallons per minute (GPM). Quality is determined by smelling, tasting and testing the water.

You will be depending on a well for your water, either one on your land or a community well that serves several properties and that may be run by a water district. Individual wells are by far the most common. No one is apt to finance your rural purchase without some proof that the water supply is adequate and potable, but this is such a critical element I advise you to pay particular attention to it. Arrange for the testing and pay for it yourself to ensure that there are absolutely no questions. Don't rely on a water test that was done previously if it is several years old. Wells go dry, and contaminants can leech into them.

Are There Water Rights?

If you plan to do a little gentleperson farming as a hobby on your spread, you will probably need to irrigate your crops. Remember the range wars in the Old West? The fights were often about water. As a result of the critical nature of this natural resource, an elaborate set of water rights laws have evolved in each state. If your parcel has water rights, they should be a matter of formal public record. Know what you are getting and what you are not, and how to protect what you have. In some cases nonuse for a certain period will result in the loss of rights.

Who Puts Out Fires?

Rural fire departments are generally of the volunteer variety, and their primary job often is to protect natural resources—not necessarily structures. Find out how far it is to the nearest fire station (sometimes meaning a truck parked in a barn) and how long it would take to respond to a fire at your house.

How Is It Taxed?

There are an incredible number of tax laws that relate to farms and ranches and what you do, or agree not to do, on them. They can apply to small parcels as well as large, so don't assume that because you are just doing a little hobby farming on a handful of acres there's no need to check. For example, if you happen to buy a piece of property that was enjoying a reduction in property taxes because the owner was growing, or refraining from growing, a particular crop and you changed the use of the land, you could be required to pay retroactive (before you owned the property) taxes.

How's the Sewage Disposal System?

Chances are that you will have an individual septic system on your property. In case you don't know how that works, it all happens underground (if everything is functioning properly). Sewage goes to a large holding tank, is broken down by a natural process (some people introduce chemicals, hoping to speed things up) and is then disbursed into what is called a leach field. That may strike you as disgusting if you've never encountered the concept before (a student in one of my real estate classes said, "Eww . . . , you mean you let your children walk on that ground?"), but it's an efficient and safe process if everything is going according to plan. However, as a matter of personal preference and based upon no scientific knowledge, I've avoided planting deep-growing tube vegetables over our leach field.

There is standard advice that is given to those with septic systems. The tanks need to be pumped periodically, and it helps if the occupants don't use a garbage disposal, since that introduces material that is tough to break down. The system can also get flooded if too much water is introduced into it by such things as interminably long showers. This means that if you are considering a place that will have several teenagers living in it, you will want to be particularly wary. You will also want to stroll in the area where the leach field is located (if you get wet shoes on a dry day, it's a bad sign), and a formal inspection by a competent firm is an absolute must.

Mobile Homes

Although the preferred term is *manufactured home*, everyone seems to understand *mobile home* better, so that's the terminology we'll use. This is the type of home you encounter on the interstate when you see a truck with flashing red lights and a sign that says "wide load," followed by two huge trailer truck rigs, each carrying half of a mobile home unit that will be erected on a permanent site. If that mobile home is permanently attached to a foundation on land that the mobile home owner also owns, it is treated as real estate. If it's in a mobile home park on rented space, it's treated as personal property. We are only interested in mobile homes as real property—as a home ownership alternative.

The Balance Sheet

Price.   It costs less to build mobile homes at a factory than it does to construct stick-built homes on-site. As a matter of fact, it costs about two-thirds less on a per-square-foot basis. Whether you buy a new mobile home from the factory and put it on a permanent foundation on a lot you purchase or opt for a preowned mobile home already set up as real property, you'll find that on average they are less expensive than most of your other choices.

Quality.   Here you need to pay close attention. There are vast differences in the quality of construction in mobile homes. As a matter of fact, there have been such serious problems that in 1976 Congress stepped in and mandated that mobile homes must be constructed in accordance with the National Manufactured Home Construction Safety Standards Act. Mobile homes built after June 14, 1976, must display a small identification plate on the outside of each unit that indicates that the unit conforms with HUD construction standards. Mobile homes must also contain other important information, including the wind and snow loads for which they were designed.

There still are thousands of pre-1976 mobile homes in use. Some estimates are as high as 50 percent of all existing units. These homes present special hazards, not the least of which relate to fire danger. For example, in one western state, over the past ten years mobile home fires accounted for 6 percent of total residential fires but for 21 percent of the deaths, with the major blame placed on the older units. The clear moral to this particular story is to avoid any mobile home not built to current HUD standards.

There's another element involved in mobile home safety that you need to consider. It is very important that when mobile homes are attached to their permanent foundations, it should be done by people who know what they are doing. Otherwise, the homes have a tendency to become unstable during heavy winds—as in blowing into the next county. While HUD has set construction standards, they don't regulate on-site installation. Because of some particularly unfortunate experiences in recent hurricanes, new standards are being developed by HUD to improve the ability of mobile homes to withstand high winds, but all of that has not yet been sorted out. If you plan to buy a mobile home located on the southeastern coast of the United States (where windstorms are common), you must pay particular attention to the quality of construction and to the method of attachment to the foundation.

● ●

Florida Shangri-La

I don't want to give the impression that all is gloom and doom with mobile homes. After all, there are over 7 million mobile home owners in the United States, so there must be something there. About half of those owners are in mobile home developments, either on rented or owned space, and the other half are on private land in rural areas. Some of the developments are quite modern and convenient.

For example, a few years ago I did a feature for a military publication on service retirees building or buying their dream homes. One empty-nester retired navy couple we featured had purchased a mobile home in an upscale Florida development. The price of the home was considerably less than a comparable stick-built home would have been. The development featured around-the-clock security, a convenient nearby shopping mall, golf just down the road, outside maintenance that was provided (which permitted the couple to travel extensively without worrying about the home front) and an active recreational and social program. The mobile homes themselves, based upon the pictures I saw and the literature I reviewed, plus the testimony of the owners, were luxurious. These were definitely two very happy campers. I'm sure they would highly recommend living in a mobile home.

● ●

Digging In

Mobile homes can be made to be quite secure and stable, with a little work and the right motivation. For example, during a year's tour in Vietnam I lived in a compound of mobile homes that had been retrofitted for a combat environment. There were reinforced concrete walls designed to withstand direct hits by incoming rockets that encased each unit up to window level. The roofs had been reinforced to withstand monsoon rain and winds. In about 300 square feet of air-conditioned living space I had a shower, kitchen, closet and combination bedroom, living room, dining room, library and den. Except for an occasional cobra slithering by the window on the concrete wall and frequent late-night visits by Macho, the largest rat I ever saw, it was a very pleasant living arrangement and quite secure. Now it would be an unusual circumstance in which you would build a five-foot concrete wall around your mobile home, but if you did, I guarantee you that baby isn't likely to go anywhere in a windstorm.

● ●

Landlording

I'll finish this discussion by suggesting an alternative that has some real potential, assuming you are temperamentally suited.

●●

Home Sweet Duplex

In 1981 I worked with a young bachelor (we'll call him Sam) who was coming to town to enter a masters program at the local university. Since that was likely to be followed by a PhD program, the probability was that he would be in the area for a few years at the minimum.

Sam therefore decided he wanted to buy a house rather than rent. We looked at many options, but what he eventually settled on was a new duplex that had just been built in a nice neighborhood conveniently located within biking distance of campus. It was constructed by the builder to attract an owner-occupant. There was an FHA construction loan on the duplex that was assumable and convertible to permanent fixed-rate, long-term financing. The price of the unit was $90,000. Sam bought it, lived in one side and rented the other side. What he really bought instead of a duplex was a two-bedroom, two-and-one-half bath, 1,200-square-foot home for $45,000 and a two-bedroom, two-bath, 1,100-square-foot rental for $45,000. The original rent was $350. It's now 12 years later. The market value of the duplex is now about $145,000, or roughly a 61 percent increase, and property is now appreciating at 10 to 12 percent per year. Rent for the unit is $775 (about a 120 percent increase) and is going up. Dr. Sam now works for the federal government and still lives in the duplex with his wife and little girl. He refinanced the FHA mortgage several years ago since it was taken out at a time when interest rates were high. He now has a 30-year, fixed-rate loan, so his payments will remain the same while rents escalate. He purchased a building lot in the nearby hills a few years ago, hired a local builder to construct his dream home and is planning to move into the new home soon. He will keep the duplex. He says rent from one side of it will cover costs there, and rent from the other side will pay for about half his monthly costs in the new home.

• •

Landlording: The Rest of the Story

It's not really that difficult to get financing for an owner-occupied rental property, although you ordinarily must put more into a down payment and your interest rates will be somewhat higher. In a duplex you will be qualified on the basis of an owner-occupant for your side, while the rental side will be considered on its investment merits and your ability to handle the inherent risks. It's not an uncommon occurrence, so if you head down this road, you won't be lonely.

Of course, the property doesn't have to be a duplex. It can be a fourplex or a 12-unit apartment house. The more rental units that are involved, the more complex financing will become. You also must establish contact early with your accountant, since you will be depreciating the rental portion of your investment and will be permitted to deduct expenses that relate to the rentals.

So what's the downside? If Dr. Sam had decided to sell his duplex in 1986, he would have taken a loss; and since he put a substantial amount down, that would have been a hard-money loss, as opposed to an equity loss. Local property values slumped and federal tax legislation was passed that made owning rental property not quite as good a deal as it had been. Of course things eventually rebounded; Dr. Sam kept upgrading the duplex by adding such things as central air; and if he sold now, he would have an impressive capital gain (which the feds would notice). In addition, not everyone is cut out to be a landlord, particularly when your tenant is on the other side of the wall. On the other hand, you would certainly be one of the few people who could pick your own neighbor and require them to pay for the privilege of living next to you.

We will have a few additional thoughts on landlording in the final chapter.

• • ▼ •

Red Flag Checklist
and Survival Strategies

1. Every time you see television coverage of disasters caused by tornadoes and hurricanes you notice that it seems to be the mobile home parks that get hit the hardest.

Strategy: The preferred term is *manufactured housing,* but when Mother Nature unloads her wind, they may more accurately be described as *mobile.* It's not that they somehow attract tempestuous weather or that God has it in for them; it's just that they are more vulnerable. It's a good idea to ensure that the unit is as well fastened to the foundation as is possible and that you are properly insured.

2. It's August, and the country home you are considering has a quaint little stream gurgling along a few feet from the back deck.

Strategy: August's quaint little stream may become January's roaring torrent. Get up to speed on such terms as *flood plain,* and have a serious talk with your insurance agent. Spend a few moments discussing local winters with potential neighbors.

3. The owner of the rural home you are considering tells you that the brown water with the unusual odor bubbling up in the corner of the backyard is actually a valuable natural-mineral-water spring.

Strategy: You might be wise to check this out with the county sanitation office. Failing septic systems sometimes exhibit the same bubbling and aromatic tendencies.

4. You've found a great little two-acre parcel in the country upon which you plan to build your dream home. The owner says it already has septic approval.

Strategy: That's encouraging, but you need to get the specifics. In situations such as these, septic approvals typically specify the size (number of bedrooms/baths) of the home that can be built. If you want to build a six-bedroom, six-bath home for your clan and the approval limits the structure to a three-bedroom, two-bath home, it's not a practical alternative for you.

5. *You locate a comfortable little duplex you can qualify for as an owner-occupant, but you aren't sure you want to live in the same building as your tenant.*

Strategy: If you can figure out a way to buy a single-family home, that is probably the better alternative for you, considering your misgivings. If it turns out that this is the *only* way you can afford a home, bite the bullet and become a live-in landlord, at least for a couple of years.

6. *You are thinking about buying a nice rural lot as a building site. It even has an old barn on it that could be restored along with an antique gas pump next to it.*

Strategy: Whistles. Bells. Roman candles. You may be looking at underground gas tanks. That could mean big, big trouble. They leak; they contaminate ground water; they have to be removed. It's incredibly expensive. Look elsewhere or get an environmental assessment.

7. *A piece of rural property you look at has the notation "tax deferral" on the listing.*

Strategy: There are some extremely complex laws regarding farm property. You must find out the specifics. If you change the use of the property, you could be hit with a huge tax bill.

8. *A rural lot that's on the market has an easement from an adjoining property for its septic leach field.*

Strategy: This is not all that uncommon, but make sure you know what you're getting. That would mean you would have two leach fields—your own and your neighbor's. You could obviously not build any structure over either, and the potential for system failure is always there. You also want to make certain your neighbors know to have their septic tank pumped regularly.

9. *A rural subdivision had 100 lots that were sold for development. There is one remaining.*

Strategy: I would have to ask why 99 buyers chose other lots. It's very possible they knew something you haven't yet found out.

10. *A real estate agent shows you a rural property that has no road access. He tells you that won't be a problem since state law requires that access be*

provided by way of an easement over the adjoining property in cases such as this.

Strategy: Sometimes a little knowledge is a dangerous thing. While many states do have such access laws, each case is judged on its merits, and even if an easement is granted, there can be a considerable delay and possible expenses in getting it.

8

$$\blacktriangledown$$

Preparing Your Game Plan

You have weighed your options and have decided that home owner-ship is definitely for you. Whether it's your first or your fifth home, you know it will require sacrifice and a long-term commitment; but you're convinced that it's worth it and you are up to it. You've balanced the books, decided about how much home you can reasonably afford, determined the type of home you'll go for, established a time frame, tightened the belt, studied up on the rules of engagement and are ready to get on with it.

If you already live in the community in which you want to buy, your job will be a little easier. If you have to do your homework from afar, it gets somewhat more complicated. We'll cover both scenarios; but whether you house hunt from near or far, here are some suggestions on how to select a real estate agent with whom to work.

Selecting a Real Estate Agent

If you skipped the Preface, let me repeat: On balance, I believe you can buy and sell homes more quickly and efficiently by working with a well-qualified real estate agent. Furthermore, in the long run it will probably save you money. Yes, there are some important qualifications and exceptions, but I did it both ways before I entered the business and

I've watched closely since I've been in the profession. That's how it seems to work out most of the time. But you do have to know the ground rules.

Which Agent?

Let's assume you decide to work within the standard seller agency relationship. It will still be to your advantage to deal with only one agent. But you may say, "If I've understood this whole thing correctly, you are suggesting that I work exclusively with someone who is representing the seller." That's correct, but I'm making the recommendation in your best interests.

First, it will be easier for you. The way the system works is that any agent can get information on practically any home in which you are interested. I will admit that I didn't know that before I started selling real estate. For example, we became aware of our current home when we drove by it while being shown another home in the neighborhood by a very competent, personable real estate agent. Unfortunately for her, she didn't mention to us that despite the fact that the home had the real estate sign of another company, she could show it to us.

Second, let's say your house hunting extends over several weeks or months. You see an ad in the paper for a place that sounds great, but the ad doesn't include the address. That's so you will have to phone the real estate company that has it listed. When you call, the person responding has one objective—to get your name and make an appointment to show you the property. The agent will probably try to establish some rapport and ask a few questions to find out how serious a buyer you are, but the appointment is the number-one objective. In many cases, if pushed to the wall, the agent will refuse to give the address. If you have established contact with your own friendly professional, you can avoid all that by simply calling and asking for the address. If you like what you see, you call back and your contact will make an appointment to show the home. That's easier for you, and the agent hopes to gain your loyalty.

• •

Picking a Winner

I can best illustrate how I suggest you pick a real estate agent by relating a personal experience. Although it involved selecting an agent to sell a home, the concept is the same. Several years ago my mother passed away, and I had to travel from Oregon to California to settle her estate. My biggest task was to sell her house. Since I had a great deal to accomplish in a limited time, I wanted to list with an agent who would do the job for me quickly and professionally. I had no personal contacts on which to rely. First, for reasons we've already discussed, I decided to work with a REALTOR®. I called several REALTOR® brokers and said I was going to list my home and wanted to hear from someone in their company with the following qualifications:

1. *The agent worked at real estate full-time.* There are real estate agents who work on a part-time basis and may be very competent, but you want to deal with someone who devotes his or her full energies to the job.

2. *The agent had the Graduate, REALTORS® Institute (GRI) professional designation.* This is a three-course sequence sponsored by state REALTOR® organizations based upon a curriculum designed by the National Association of REALTORS®. It's a sign that the REALTOR® is taking the business seriously.

3. *The agent closed over $1 million in transactions the previous year.* I forgot it was California. I should have made that at least $5 million. You want to work with successful, experienced agents. I hate to say this, since I was once a rookie REALTOR® myself, but successful experience counts. The last thing I want to hear before undergoing brain surgery is my doctor telling me how excited she is to be doing her first operation on a live human. Go with the old heads—meaning experience, not necessarily age.

In response to my calls, I interviewed three agents. All were very well qualified. The woman I chose actually had the Certified REALTOR® Specialist (CRS) professional designation, which is one step higher than the GRI. Let me tell you, she was good. We sold the house at a fair price to qualified buyers in less than three weeks.

● ●

How *Not* To Pick an Agent

For reasons that aren't completely clear to me, people choose real estate agents for some very strange reasons. "My cousin Vinnie just got his license and needed the sale to impress his parole officer" is a variant on an often-heard theme. People also seem to be attracted to working with ex-celebrities, even of the small-town variety. Former athletes or coaches who go into real estate, for example, are typically inundated with business from folks anxious to rub shoulders with the formerly famous. There is nothing to say that these folks won't do a terrific job, but it's just that there are much better criteria to use when choosing a professional with whom to work. My top two criteria are honesty and competence.

You will note that with my California experience I had no one to ask for recommendations. That still remains a valuable strategy, and it is how most people choose their agents. But there are cautions. The most important is to make certain the person you ask has standards similar to your own and can recognize professional competence (and incompetence). In addition, never ask someone for a referral who has a personal interest in the recommendation. (Remember cousin Vinnie.)

Selling Your Current Castle

If you own a home that you must sell before you can buy a new one, it can pose a problem. Sellers don't like to accept an offer contingent upon the buyers selling their house. It's really a timing problem, and it can be quite complicated. If your move is definite and you must sell your home to afford another, your best course of action is to shape it up, price it right, list it with an agent who has demonstrated an ability to sell homes in your neighborhood and find a buyer before you become one. If you have a sale on your home pending, sellers will be more receptive to an offer contingent upon the actual closing of the transaction. Astute real estate agents and attorneys representing the seller will, however, check with the escrow company or lawyer handling your sale to verify that it is in fact a solid transaction with no serious contingencies.

If you will buy a new home *only* if you can sell your present home, then your approach may be a little more relaxed. Real estate agents prefer working with motivated (desperate) sellers, since they tend to price the property more realistically and are much easier to work with in the negotiation process.

Breaking the Code

In conducting your research, I advise reviewing the real estate sections of newspapers. The major benefit is that you will get a good overview of how much money it is apt to take to buy the type of property you want. This can also help in detecting good (and bad) deals. You must be familiar with the standard buzzwords and what they really mean. Here are just a few:

> *"Owner desperate!"* This means the owner is desperate. Really desperate.
> *"Asking price: $199,000."* The key word is *asking*. That's telling you the price is very soft.
> *"Submit all offers."* They haven't had any and would really like to see one.
> *"Price just reduced!"* They overpriced the home and didn't luck out with a quick sale. It may still be overpriced.
> *"Starter home."* No one who has ever owned a home before would consider it. Okay, it could mean it's a cute little cottage just perfect for you.
> *"Owner financing available."* This probably means that the home is owned free and clear and the seller wants to be the banker. This could be a good deal, but sometimes it means the property has flaws that a normal lender wouldn't accept.
> *"Easy commute. Seven miles as the crow flies."* If you aren't a crow, it's 35 miles on a dirt road.
> *"Historic property."* It has been on the market so long it finally qualifies for that status.

Real estate advertising at one time was even more creative and entertaining than it is now. Federal legislation has cut down on the latitude ad writers enjoy, particularly as it relates to financing and fair housing. The restrictions have actually made the ads much less informative in some instances. For example, there are now certain taboo words and phrases that may not be used on the theory that they indicate a possible discrimination against certain protected classes. For example, you aren't likely to see descriptions such as "exclusive neighborhood," "great family living" or "terrific school district." If you're looking for any of those things, you will have to do personal investigation.

Doing Your Homework

Even though for convenience I've broken the following discussion down into two categories—out-of-town buyers and hometown buyers—it will be valuable for you to review all the information, no matter where you are located.

Out-of-Town Buyers

Your challenge is to get to know the community in which you will live. If it's a big city, you will want to know how to narrow your focus. If you are relocating because of a job, you may have some help from your company. If that's the case, great, but we will assume you are pretty much on your own. Even if you aren't, it's important to know how the process works because you are still going to be making the important decisions (like which house to buy). Here's a suggested plan of attack.

Write for Information.   Most cities have an aggressive chamber of commerce that is anxious to spread the good word about the virtues of their community. Write to the chamber of commerce where you are headed and ask for information, including data about real estate. You will get a packet from them, and if the real estate people there are on the ball, you will also get phone calls from agents anxious to help you.

During those calls you will be asked several questions, some directly and others more subtly. The typical questions are as follows: "When do you plan to relocate?", "Where will you be working, or are you retired?", "What type of home will you be looking for?", "What type of home are you in now?", "What price range will you be looking in?", "How many in your family?", "Do you have your home listed for sale now and if yes, at what price?", "Do you or your family have any special needs, such as a requirement to be near public transportation?", "Do you have school-age children?" and "When will you be in town for a house-hunting trip?"

There are other questions real estate people love to ask to determine whether you are a qualified, serious buyer, but they won't want to scare you off. Their goal at this juncture is to establish rapport and determine how hot a prospect you are. If they impress you enough to do business with them, they figure they can fill in the details when they meet with you. I suggest you reveal only sufficient detail to enable the agents to respond with the type of information that will be most helpful to you. Don't divulge more than you need to.

Ask for representative samples of listings. Some may send only information about their own listings, while others may provide you with listing material from other offices as well. (Give those who do that extra points.) Make sure you get a map of the city that shows where such facilities as hospitals, schools, libraries and parks are located. If public transportation is important to you, ask for transit system material. Also ask for information about and a map of surrounding areas that may be within commuting distance. Don't be bashful, and don't worry about getting duplicate material.

Since your goal is to choose one REALTOR® with whom to work, start making judgments. Ask the agent to include a business card in the packet. Check the card to ensure that the agent is a REALTOR® and whether or not they have any advance professional designations, such as GRI or CRS. Many of the top producers will have things written on their cards (e.g., "Member of the Bizillion Dollar Club" or "Member of Top Producer Council"). Some will have personal brochures that describe their accomplishments and virtues in full color.

Subscribe to the Local Newspaper. If time permits, subscribe to the local newspaper for a few months before you move. In addition to giving you good insight into local happenings, the newspaper will contain real estate advertising. You need to study that section very carefully, for you can start to get an idea of comparative home prices and desirable areas. You will also get a good feel for who the active, aggressive real estate brokers are.

Write Real Estate Brokers.   If the chamber of commerce letter doesn't result in many responses from real estate companies, drop a line to a few of the brokers whose newspaper ads look promising and follow the general guidance we discussed previously.

House-Hunting Trips.   There are occasions where a buyer makes a premove visit for the express purpose of purchasing a home. I advise against such a visit if you have other realistic choices, since making a major decision after investigating for just a few days can be risky. Another option is a premove visit just to survey the housing situation, which I prefer because it takes off the pressure. Another option is to move and rent temporary lodgings while house hunting.

We will cover specific house-hunting strategies in Chapter 11, but I must emphasize that if you do indeed travel to your new hometown in advance of the move specifically to purchase a home, you really must be prepared and must steel yourself to make very important decisions under pressure.

Let the agent know that you plan to be there to buy a house, assuming you find one you like and can afford, so a schedule can be arranged to spend the time needed with you to get the job done. Typically, you will get very good treatment from real estate agents who know you are on a homebuying trip, including any help you need with hotel reservations, travel arrangements and car rentals.

No matter how royally you are treated or how close the real estate agent sticks to you, arrange for time to yourself where you can cruise the community strictly on your own. For your agent's peace of mind (assuming you are satisfied), assure her that if, during your self-guided tour, you see a home that interests you that is for sale by another real estate company, you will contact her to show it to you.

Hometown Buyers

While your job will be easier from a logistical standpoint than if you live out of town, you still have your work cut out for you. The major advantage is that you can look at actual homes that are for sale on a more or less relaxed, pressure-free basis until you're actually ready to throw your hat in the ring.

Remember, to do this most efficiently, work with *one* real estate agent. If there have been any homes listed and sold in your neighborhood in the past year or so, you will have had an opportunity to observe some agents firsthand. If the real estate people where you live are on the ball, a few of them would have knocked on your door to introduce themselves and let you know they had a listing around the corner. They would have contacted you again to invite you to the open house, and most assuredly they would have let you know when the home was sold.

Finally, if you know anyone from a title company, a lending institution or an attorney's office, ask for a recommendation. Trust me. They know the local agents very well.

Red Flag Checklist and Survival Strategies

1. You would like to buy a home near a parochial school in the city to which you are relocating but are having trouble getting the information you need from real estate agents.

Strategy: Revealing such information may be viewed by some REALTORS® as sensitive because of federal fair housing laws. You will probably get better results by working through the appropriate church.

2. The real estate agent you make an appointment with to show you a modest two-bedroom starter home shows up in a Rolls Royce with a chauffeur.

Strategy: That would make me a little nervous, although engaging in conspicuous consumption isn't necessarily a disqualifying character trait. I am more interested in other personal qualities but would somehow wonder if the agent would feel motivated enough to spend sufficient time on my dinky little transaction.

3. The real estate agent who volunteered to meet your incoming flight for your house-hunting trip arrives 30 minutes late and in a car that smells as though he just returned from a successful fishing trip.

Strategy: That would do it for me, short of a great excuse like he had a collision with a fish truck on the way to the airport. If an agent hasn't got his stuff together enough to be on time, I can't believe he will do a professional job for me.

4. You are moving across country and have to sell your current home. A local broker advises that it should pose no problem on the other end as long as you make any offer contingent upon selling your current home.

Strategy: Let me ask you this question: Would you accept an offer on your home and take it off the market contingent upon the buyer selling his or her home? Unless your home had been on the market for a long time with absolutely no offers or expressions of interest, I would advise you not to make such an offer. Sell. Then buy.

5. You attend an open house at a new home in a subdivision and the agent hosting it tells you that his real estate company is the only one authorized to sell in that subdivision.

Strategy: That happens sometimes, but it is the exception. Most builders want maximum exposure and will "co-op" with all brokers. Check with the real estate agent with whom you have elected to work.

6. There are three high schools in the city to which you plan to move. You want to make certain that you get in the right district for your daughter to participate in the gymnastics program at Washington High.

Strategy: This requires serious personal investigation. In some places school district lines change rather frequently, and in others students may be transported to a school across town. Check with school district officials for the latest information, and limit your search to appropriate neighborhoods.

7. As you ride around your hometown surveying the real estate situation, you notice one large neighborhood with an unusual number of For Sale signs.

Strategy: It may be just an incredible coincidence that the whole neighborhood decided to sell at the same time. More likely, this could spell trouble, so make sure you investigate. There are times when such things as impending roadway construction, rezoning, expensive mandatory sewer hookups or a large nearby commercial development will cause homeowners to conclude that the neighborhood isn't going to be as livable as it once was, and they decide to pull out. Panic selling occasionally occurs. If the nature of the upcoming change is dramatic and is perceived by owners as undesirable, then potential buyers will view it the same way. The standard technical advice in situations such as this is, "Don't touch it with a ten-foot pole."

8. You are very impressed with a real estate agent you meet at an open house and think she might be the right choice for you to work with in shopping for a house. However, she is a teacher in a local school and sells real estate part-time.

Strategy: As a rule, I recommend against working with part-time agents. Selling real estate is a demanding profession and requires dedication and full attention to do it justice. However, I admit that I have encountered an occasional part-timer who accomplishes more in 15 hours a week than some full-timers do in 50. Furthermore, as a buyer it is more likely that your part-timer will serve you adequately since you will be able to look at homes on a flexible schedule. Check to ensure that she is currently putting transactions together successfully. If the vibes are right, if you are convinced of her competence and professionalism and if you have encountered no full-time agent whom you prefer, I guess I could bend the rules. If she is a school teacher and it's August, you've even got her full-time!

9. After initial contact with a REALTOR® with whom you were very impressed, follow-up contacts are coming from someone who identifies herself as the REALTOR®'s assistant.

Strategy: This is not necessarily a sign that your REALTOR® doesn't think you are worthy of her individual attention, although it may have been better judgment for her to have established a more lasting rapport with you before she called in help. A growing trend for very successful REALTORS® is to hire help to do routine activities. Some assistants have licenses and others do not. Having an assistant (or several) is actually a good sign, presuming the REALTOR® is astute enough to follow up to ensure that the assistants do things properly.

10. A neighborhood in the town in which you are interested borders on what you hear referred to as a "natural area."

Strategy: The term *natural area* can mean that the zoning is such that the land can never be built upon. If that's the case, it is a plus for the neighborhood. The term, however, is often used very loosely, and sometimes it's employed to give a false impression.

9

▼

Real Estate Agents:
The Good, the Bad, the Ugly

It was a tumultuous time on the University of California, Berkeley, campus in the Spring of 1970, where one sunny afternoon things really erupted. As usual, the epicenter was at Sproul Plaza. As TV cameras rolled to capture Berkeley's riot de jour for the six o'clock news, students, police, the National Guard and an assortment of frenzied street people ran helter-skelter, screaming and shouting in a haze of tear gas. I watched, as in the midst of it all in the Plaza, oblivious to what was going on around him, sat a gaunt-looking middle-aged man with thinning long hair and a beard, clothed in nothing but a pair of cutoff jeans. He was sitting with legs crossed in a Gandhilike position with his eyes toward the heavens and his arms outstretched, plaintively asking over and over, "Who am I? Who am I?"

There are a lot of real estate agents who seem to be asking the same question right now as they try to figure out the role they are supposed to play in working with homebuyers. Traditional, comfortable ways of doing business are being challenged, news laws are being passed and it's all extremely unsettling. But here's the good news. It really doesn't make that much difference to you if they know who *they* are as long as you know who *you* are. You will be able to get along very well with them, no matter what the formal agency relationship is.

Real Estate Agents: The Good

Under the best of circumstances, you will probably become very friendly with the real estate agent with whom you work and will be extremely impressed with the myriad of details that get taken care of in a professional, highly competent fashion. Whether a seller's agent or buyer's agent, you will likely develop a mutual trust and respect, and several years from now when you decide to sell your home, that's the person you are apt to call to list it for you. There is absolutely no problem with that scenario. For those of us in the business, it's what has made the profession enjoyable and satisfying.

Communicate and Prosper

To help ensure that things turn out the way I've described, you must communicate very clearly with your REALTOR® at every step. In just a moment we will describe some important matters that will be covered during your first formal meeting, but there's one topic we should discuss first that merits your special attention. From your first contact to your last, you need to stress that whatever home you eventually buy must have a good location.

Location, Location, Location.   You already know the answer to the question, "What are the three most important factors in determining the value of a specific piece of real estate?" They are location, ditto, ditto. Here's why. Let's say you find the home you want, but it doesn't have a fenced backyard—a must for your toddlers. Within reason, you can change any of the physical features of the home. What you cannot change is its location. Here's an example.

• •

The Midnight Callers

I was once working with a couple from out of state who were coming to our local area to retire. I located a nice little home on a quiet street in a well-tended neighborhood that I thought would be perfect for them. It had a large backyard with a high wooden fence that bordered the rear of a large grocery store. The fence blocked the view of the store completely, and it was quite a tranquil setting. What I didn't know, and what my customer pointed out to me (he was a meat cutter), is that deliveries to grocery stores often occur late at night and are typically made to the rear of the store. He further assured me that big trucks make lots of noise and that drivers and store personnel don't always use their "inside voices" while unloading. The house itself was perfect for them. The location was not, and they would have been stuck with it. Of less importance is the fact that I would have had some very unhappy customers who would have volunteered their opinion of my professional expertise for years to come to anyone who would listen.

• •

Some matters regarding location are personal (like how far it is to your work). You may have to make a judgment call if there's to be a trade-off (e.g., great little house but a long commute). Then there is the standard "no brainer" advice, such as "Don't buy next to the garbage dump, under the off-ramp of the freeway or next to the old artillery range at the former U.S. Army base north of town," but I'm certain you can reach conclusions like that without much guidance.

So what's the number-one location factor for residential property? Experienced real estate professionals say it relates to traffic. They say to avoid buying on or near a busy street since that will mean noise, unpleasant and unhealthy fumes and potential danger for kiddies who wander and for those of us who aren't nimble enough to get across the street before the Don't Walk sign starts flashing.

From an investment standpoint, here is the most important reason you should insist upon a good location. When you become a seller, as you probably will eventually, the location of your house will largely determine how easy it is to sell and how much you get for it.

Your Initial Meeting. Perhaps you have had several contacts with the agent previously by telephone or through correspondence and may have even met briefly. This meeting is your first face-to-face formal meeting, which will often take place in the real estate broker's office. There will probably be a large, detailed map of the city and the surrounding area on the wall to help you get oriented as well as other literature about the local community. If you're from out of town, this will be particularly helpful. There may even be elaborate pictorial displays of properties, including videos of some of them.

By this time you have provided basic information and have done a great deal of work on your own, including getting prequalified and making preliminary decisions on your housing preferences. Depending upon how much contact you have had and what is already known, the agent will have several objectives at this meeting. Among them, will be to determine or to confirm the following:

- *Exactly what type of home you are looking for.* You will be able to recognize this step by questions such as "Exactly what type of home are you looking for?" Be prepared to discuss style, size, location and price.

  You already know you are going to stress the importance of location in general, but you should also mention any special preferences and specific needs you may have. For families with school-age children, schools are often an extended topic of discussion. Even if this is not of personal concern to you at the moment, make it clear that you insist upon a home in a quality school district, from elementary to secondary. That will have a big impact on the value of your home.

  It will be helpful for both you and your agent if you compose a specific list of the features you would like in your home. The list can include everything from an eat-in kitchen to a fenced backyard to a fireplace to a double garage. Jot down everything you can think of on your wish list. Then go back and decide which features are essential and which are merely desirable. It will be helpful to assign a numerical rating to each feature with ten being the most important and one the least.

  During your discussion the agent will probably ask questions such as "Why is a house with space for a home office important to you?" The purpose will be to determine your basic motivations and your true lifestyle preferences. With that information it will be easier to offer alternate suggestions if the precise home you want is not realistically available or if there's a solution that may not have occurred to you.

- *Whether or not you are qualified financially.* Homebuyers typically know how much home they can afford, but not always. Real estate agents have learned from hard experience to qualify buyers before they spend their time and gas showing them homes. There is no profession where the phrase "time is money" applies more. Real estate agents only get paid when they close a deal, so the real pros make sure they work exclusively with qualified, motivated buyers. Think how impressed the agent will be when you reveal that you have already been to the bank and prequalified for a loan. Beyond disclosing that fact, don't get into all the details of your vast financial empire, even if you are working with a buyer's agent.

- *How much you have for your initial investment.* Some real estate agents consider the term *down payment* tacky and fear that if they use it, you will immediately freeze up, since it will evoke visions of parting with a large chunk of your bank account and committing yourself to decades of indentured servitude to a lending institution. Whatever you call it, how much cash you have up front is considered a good indicator of how serious a buyer you are. I suggest you speak in general terms, such as "We've qualified based upon our 10 percent down."

- *Whether you have to sell another home before you buy.* If that is the case, the major focus will immediately shift to the sale of your home. Do you have it on the market? Are you trying to sell it yourself, or is it listed with a broker? Is there an offer on it? Is it in the process of closing? How much equity do you have in it? If it's located in the same town and is not yet on the market, you can anticipate a pitch to list it. If it's in another town, you will be encouraged to list it. It's possible the agent will want to put you in contact with a broker there, since that would result in a referral fee when the home sells.

- *How motivated a buyer you are.* You will probably be asked the question "How long have you been looking?" If your answer is "since 1981," chances are your meeting will be a little shorter than you had originally anticipated. On the other hand, if you say "We've sold our condo in Aspen, and we want to be settled in our new home in time for the opening of the school year in six weeks," anticipate a sudden flush in your agent's face and frenzied activity. If that Aspen condo was twice as expensive as the average home in the local area, you can probably also expect a quick reminder that to avoid paying a whopping tax on your gain, you will have to invest in a home of equal or greater value.

Although the agent would also like to ask "Will you be able to recognize the home you want when you see it?" and "Do you have the intestinal fortitude to make a tough decision in a timely fashion?", those questions will probably be deferred and those judgments made based on other more subtle inputs.

- *Who makes the decisions.* If there are two of you and during the interview one of you naps frequently and stares blankly out the window when awake, the agent will conclude that the comatose partner is not going to play an important role in the decision-making process. It is much preferable that everyone be alert and interested and ask probing questions.

- *Whether you are working with another real estate broker.* There are practical reasons for this question. Professional ethics dictate that if you have seen a property with another agent, then the REALTOR® interviewing you will not show it again and will not work with you on buying that property. There are methods of working things like this out between brokers, but it's best to avoid that situation. As I've suggested, it is far better to decide on one agent before you actually start looking at any homes.

At the conclusion of your initial meeting, you should be confident that you have chosen the right REALTOR®, and the REALTOR® should be satisfied that you are a serious enough prospect to pile into the Mercedes or Volkswagen Bug, as the case may be, and start showing homes.

It is here that your agent will have an important but delicate job to perform: to convince you that you aren't the only person in town looking at homes. Many buyers operate as if that were the case. Here's the problem.

Working with Fast Burners

If you follow my suggestion and insist that your agent be a full-time, productive REALTOR® with the GRI or CRS designation, you will be working with one of the most successful agents on the local scene. "Ten percent of the agents do 90 percent of the business" is the saying in the trade, and it's essentially an accurate description of how things work. Your agent will be one of the 10 percent. That means a lot of thought has gone into deciding which homes to show you. These homes will be the best choices available in your price range.

Other competing agents in that elite 10 percent group will also be working with buyers whose needs are similar to yours. These successful agents tend to focus in on the same properties, and they *only* work with qualified buyers. That means that if you see something you want, you must make a decision and make an offer. Your agent will probably try to point this situation out to you but will not want to give you the impression that you are being hustled. That's why it is important for you to do all your preliminary research faithfully. Then when you see the house you want, you will have the self-confidence to make a decision.

Real Estate Agents: The Bad and the Ugly

To borrow from a well-known literary comparison, when real estate agents are good, they can be very, very good; but when they are bad—well, you know. As a well-informed participant, you will be in a position to judge good from bad and act accordingly. But just to complete your education, we need to spend some time on a few tricks of the trade that some agents use.

• • ▼ •

Red Flag Checklist and Survival Strategies

1. You have a first-grader in the family and want to be within safe walking distance of schools.

Strategy: I knew a family once with the same goal. In July they bought a home across the street from the local elementary school. It was quiet and the school was convenient. In October the school was still convenient, but the streets were crawling with little ones and the noise level from the playground was deafening. You may want to consider a place a few blocks away.

2. Your real estate agent asks if you would consider a home in which the double garage has been converted into a nice family room.

Strategy: Most people want a garage for their cars, even though it may eventually get filled with so many miscellaneous family treasures that they have to park them in the driveway. As a general rule, I would advise against converting a garage or buying a home where this has been done.

3. *You meet an agent who is hosting an open house and love the home but not the agent. You want to make an offer through a* REALTOR® *with whom you've been working in the traditional seller agency relationship.*

Strategy: In such situations it's always good to start the conversation with something like "I would love to look at the house, but I should tell you I'm working with Sue Smith at Golden Realty." That shouldn't pose a problem, but don't let the agent pile you in the car and start showing you other houses.

4. *The* REALTOR® *with whom you are meeting asks if you have anyone who could cosign on the mortgage loan.*

Strategy: That's a pretty good indication that the REALTOR® doesn't think you can qualify for a loan on your own, or at least the size of the loan needed to buy homes you will be shown. You must review your financial status and make sure the REALTOR® knows what you are qualified for.

5. *You want a country property but insist that it must be reached by paved roads. An agent tells you of a development that has gravel roads but has just formed a road district to pave them.*

Strategy: That's great, but it could turn out to be very expensive. The homeowners in the development may be assessed a pro-rata share for the paving. You should get the hard figures on this before you proceed. The paving will increase the value of the property considerably.

6. *The real estate agent you are working with tells you that a property you're interested in is just outside the city limits.*

Strategy: That could mean that city services, most notably sewer and water lines, will be extended to the property in the future. That would result in an assessment against the property that could amount to several thousand dollars. Check with the city to see if anything is in the works.

7. You and your spouse have decided that as empty nesters, you want to sell your home and move into something smaller. You've been looking for six years and still haven't found a place that both of you can agree on.

Strategy: It isn't uncommon for one spouse to be much more motivated to move than the other. What you may have here is a failure to communicate. It would be worthwhile to honestly assess your housing goals. It's hard to imagine that you couldn't find at least one suitable empty-nester home in six years.

8. A home that fits the criteria you've given your real estate agent is being officially considered as historic property.

Strategy: The rules vary from state to state on an owner's rights and obligations on property that has an historic designation. You could get a tax break. You may also have to hold the house open to the public at specified times, and you will probably not be able to alter its appearance. Find out what the rules are in your community and your state.

9. You notice that in lining up prospective homes for you to consider, all of them are listings of the real estate agent's office.

Strategy: When real estate brokers sell their own listings they make more money because they don't have to split the commission with another broker. That's good for the broker but bad for you. You want to see the best listings, no matter whose they are. Be assertive.

10. You are intrigued by a flyer describing a home but notice that it includes the phrase "located on a flag lot."

Strategy: A *flag lot* is generally a single lot facing a street that has been divided into two lots with one lot in the rear that has no street frontage. The pole of the flag represents the roadway access to the back lot. These lots are not considered as desirable as lots with roadway frontage, although it depends on the actual size and configuration.

10

•••••▼•••••

Games Real Estate Agents Play

There are two basic philosophies real estate agents seem to follow in dealing with homebuyers. We'll call them Theory P (for *professionalism*) and Theory M (for *manipulation*).

Theory P

The most prevalent philosophy, and the one you are most likely to encounter, is as follows: You, the homebuyer, have a challenge—to find the home that meets your needs and is within your financial capability. The real estate agent's job is to work with you diligently, honestly and patiently in helping you solve your housing problem. When and if everything works out to your satisfaction as well as the seller's, the agent gets paid. You aren't going to be pushed, prodded, pressured or manipulated. Unless and until you prove conclusively to the contrary, you will be treated as a serious, qualified buyer capable of making a decision when one is called for. At the end of the whole exercise, the highest compliment you can pay the agent will be to say something like "You handled everything in a most professional manner." That also means you will probably be saying nice things about the REALTOR® to friends and acquaintances. The majority of a veteran real estate agent's business comes from satisfied past customers, clients and referrals. That doesn't happen by accident.

Theory M

There is, however, a competing position. Those who advocate and practice this position view you as lovable but indecisive and are convinced that in your own best interests they must employ specific manipulative sales techniques to get you to make the proper decision (i.e., purchase the home the agent decides best meets your needs). Unfortunately, it is this point of view new agents almost universally encounter in texts and training programs, and it takes awhile for some of them to get over it. Some never do. Others get really good at it.

Here's the philosophy in a nutshell, given as advice to real estate agent hopefuls by Ira Gribin, a former president of the National Association of REALTORS® in *The Real Estate Handbook* (Dow Jones Irwin 1989): "The function of a salesperson is to motivate clients to do something that if left to themselves, they probably would not do. The salesperson must have the courage to help another person come to a conclusion for his or her ultimate benefit."

As a consumer, I prefer to be given credit for the ability to decide for myself what is of ultimate benefit to me. I also like to be treated as though I can reach a rational decision on my own without the generous and courageous help of a real estate agent (or a car salesperson or insurance agent). In this business the word *help* is often synonymous with *manipulation*. At a minimum, it can be a very fine line. As a matter of fact, Tom Hopkins, one of the best-known real estate trainers in the nation, says the following in his book, *How To Master the Art of Listing and Selling Real Estate* (Hopkins 1991): "There's a very fine line between a professional salesperson and a con man." Unfortunately, that line sometimes gets crossed when closing techniques are used.

Getting to "Yes"

In sales terminology *closing* means doing whatever is needed to get the customer's signature on the purchase order—in this instance, getting you to sign the offer to buy a house. When you sign an offer, the process begins that could, if successfully completed, result in a payday for the real estate agent. The more time that is spent with you to realize that goal, the less time is spent with other prospective buyers. If it never happens at all, it means that all the effort expended on you was wasted— except for the pleasure of your company, of course.

But What about Agency?

Can you expect different treatment if you sign on a buyer's agent? Perhaps, but remember that no matter what the agency relationship is, the transaction will still have to close before any agent gets paid. Noncontingent fees, where agents get paid no matter whether the transaction closes or not, are practically unheard of in homebuying. You can see, therefore, why there is a real motivation to get you to formally commit by signing on the proverbial dotted line. Thus, there might occasionally be just the slightest temptation to expedite the entire process by using some well-timed, battle-tested sales techniques. That being the case, and since at this very moment there may be fledgling real estate agents in your hometown who are being drilled on how to use such techniques effectively, we will spend a few moments describing some of them to you. We'll use the following story to illustrate.

• •

Sign Here. Press Hard

Imagine that you are a single mother named Bonnie who, with your son Claude, has just relocated to a pleasant little university town. As a professional, you are financially qualified to buy a home and intend to do so as soon as you are satisfied that you know the new environment well enough. You have prequalified and have established contact with a very active and successful local REALTOR® who has the GRI designation. She has already shown you a few homes, and you're confident that she will locate one you like and can afford. You are very comfortable working in the conventional seller agency arrangement, and you've touched base with a local attorney.

You decide to take Claude for a weekend trip to the coast. On the way back you pass a new home development on the outskirts of town. It's actually closer to your work than the place you are currently renting. You stop and tour the model homes. They really look promising, so you swing by the sales office for literature and meet Herb, a sales agent for the builder. You tell him that you are already working with an agent, but he informs you that his company is the exclusive representative of the builder. He is very articulate and helpful, so you decide to let him give you the information you need.

Before you know it, you have narrowed your preference to one house and are actually thinking about buying it. Your better judgment tells you not to jump into anything, so you defer a final decision until you can talk to your real estate agent. Herb, a charter member of the Theory M school, uses every closing technique ever devised to get you to sign up. Here are some old standards Herb might try.

• •

The Ben Franklin Close

This standard close is also called the balance sheet close. It typically occurs after you have discussed the pros and cons of buying the house. The selling agent will suggest that you follow the same procedure that Ben Franklin used when he was faced with a tough decision. (For example, Herb might say, "I've always considered Ben Franklin one of our wisest men, haven't you, Bonnie?") Shrewd old Ben simply drew a line down the middle of a piece of paper and put the facts favoring the decision on the right and those against it on the left. You will get help with the right-hand side and will be on your own for the left. Unless your agent was a slow learner during initial training and has failed to master this art, the factors favoring the purchase of the home will far outweigh those against it. He may very well be working from a carefully rehearsed script from which he has been instructed not to deviate ("Okay, Bonnie, let's tally up these columns and see what we've got here."), so don't interrupt if you want to get the benefit of the full presentation.

The Order Blank Close

You will need to pay close attention to spot this type of close. The agent will have a clipboard on which there are a stack of papers. He will ask a lot of questions and take a lot of notes. After a time, you notice that what you thought were notes are actually entries on an official offer-to-purchase form. The idea is to get you so accustomed to answering routine questions that you will automatically fall into line and answer the biggies, such as "How would you like to take title to your new home?" (This is sometimes called the assumptive close.) You may find it difficult to believe that people actually fall for things like this in the real world, but in the hands of a master, such tactics can be very effective.

Reductio Ad Absurdum (Reduction to the Absurd)

This tactic will typically be used if you seem to want the house but say something like "the price is $5,000 too much." After getting you to agree that price is the only thing standing in the way of making an offer, the salesperson will ask how long you think you might live in the home. Let's say you respond, "Oh, probably ten years or so." If the agent is really cheeky, he will give you a piece of paper and a pencil and ask you to do the calculations yourself—with his help. Otherwise, the agent will do them. Either way, the object is to show you that for a miserable few pennies a day (the $5,000 divided by your ten-year expected tenure in the house), you would be willing to deprive yourself (and in Bonnie's case, little Claude) of the joys and pleasures of owning this incredible home.

The Take-Away Close

This is not to be confused with the classic bait and switch technique, where you advertise one item and then switch to another when the customer shows up. Here's how it works.

Let's say Bonnie seemed really interested in one of the new homes being shown to her. Suddenly Herb stops in midsentence and says, "I've just had a horrible thought. I'm not absolutely certain that the American Dream model on Serenity Circle that you and little Claude have so obviously fallen in love with is going to be available for sale. I'll have to do some checking with the builder on that. I heard he may be building that one for his mother." Bonnie's heart races as Herb retreats to the other side of the room to call the head office. After he engages in an extended, animated discussion with the person on the other end of the line, he returns with a relieved look and this incredibly good news: "Well, it was tough, Bonnie, but the builder has agreed to sell you that one if you buy it today. He will tell his mother she will just have to wait a few more months. Sign here. Press hard. There are several copies."

This is a dynamite technique. Nothing motivates a buyer more quickly than thinking they may not be able to get something they want—even if they haven't yet decided that they really want it. The dream of every agent is to encounter other prosperous-looking buyers coming in the front door to look at a home they've just finished showing you.

This routine is so effective that it's one of the most frequently used, and abused, of the manipulative techniques. It's also the reason that really conscientious agents may seem a little self-conscious when they try to counsel you that there are, in fact, other buyers out there looking at the same properties, and if you don't wish to be disappointed, you need to be decisive.

The Whipped-Dog Close

There are many other closing techniques (one book lists 32). There also are what are called *minor closes*, in which you will be asked a lot of unimportant questions just to get you in the habit of talking and saying yes. If absolutely everything fails, the agent may resort to the lost-soul or whipped-dog close. Herb might say something like this: "Bonnie, I apologize for being such a terrible salesman. It's obvious that the American Dream model on Serenity Circle is the perfect home for you and little Claude. It is clearly all my miserable fault that I haven't been able to demonstrate that to you. Just so I don't make the same mistake again and deprive another family of the once-in-a-lifetime opportunity of owning a home here in Heavenly Valley subdivision, would you please share with me what I did wrong? Please be honest with me." The idea is that you will be so sympathetic that you may reveal an objection you had previously kept secret. If that happens, Herb could zero in on that and use his close-on-an-objection technique, as demonstrated in the following story.

● ●

What Would It Take?

Shopping for a new automobile is not most people's favorite activity, simply because they so frequently encounter salespeople who are masters at the art of manipulative selling. I share that view but thought I had the answer the last time I went shopping for a car. When I first encountered the salesman, I said, "I would really appreciate it if we could skip all the preliminaries and you could just tell me what's the best price you can offer me on this new Guzzler 3000. You see, I'm a real estate agent and I am familiar with all the sales approaches." He put his hand on my shoulder, looked incredibly sincere and responded with "Right, Ken, I want to thank you for sharing that with me. I can't tell you what a genuine pleasure it is to work with another successful sales professional such as yourself. But tell me, Ken, before we go any further, from one pro to another, what kind of a deal would it take to get you to buy that Guzzler 3000 today?"

I accepted the inevitable and went through the usual routine, including the referral to the sales manager for a final last-ditch pitch before I walked off the lot. The chances are excellent that you will have a much better experience in dealing with real estate agents in your house-hunting venture. But just in case, it's not a bad idea to be prepared.

● ●

▼ ●

Red Flag Checklist and Survival Strategies

1. *As you are looking at a new home, a real estate agent says to you, "Would you like to meet at three o'clock to write up the contract, or would four o'clock be more convenient?"*

Strategy: You just encountered the alternative-of-choice close. Both alternatives are great for the salesperson; neither may be acceptable to you. You are permitted to answer "none of the above."

2. *In looking at one home, you encounter a woman in the kitchen who looks remarkably like Betty Crocker, cooking the best-smelling bread you've ever experienced.*

Strategy: We'll chalk this up to coincidence, but there are some home-marketing experts who counsel homesellers that great smells coming from the kitchen are a terrific turn-on for potential buyers.

3. *You are discussing a possible offer on a home on Elmwood Street with a real estate broker back at the real estate office. Another agent rushes in unannounced and excitedly asks the broker, "Hey, Sam, is that listing on Elmwood still available?"*

Strategy: Have you ever heard the word *shill?* In carnival talk it means a confederate of a con man who pretends to be interested in a product to motivate someone else to buy it. No, we're not accusing the broker of doing that. However . . .

4. *You have prequalified for a loan that, with your down payment, permits you to buy a home with a maximum price of $200,000. Your real estate agent suggests looking at homes priced as high as $225,000.*

Strategy: If you do that, you will be living on the edge; but you could always offer $200,000 for that $225,000 home. The caution here is that you may see something you really want that is just slightly out of your price range but that tempts you to resort to desperate measures to buy it. That wouldn't necessarily disappoint the agent, who would make more as a result.

5. *The first three homes your real estate agent shows you are real dogs, and you're getting very discouraged. The fourth one, however, looks terrific by comparison.*

Strategy: You have probably been subjected to the old "Beauty and the Beast" routine, which is to show several ugly sisters first and follow with Cinderella. If this happens, have a heart-to-heart talk with your real estate agent.

6. *When showing you a home, it's clear that it is the first time the agent has seen the inside.*

Strategy: You're dealing with a real amateur if this happens. It would be understandable, however, if the agent preceded it with "I haven't been able to preview the inside of this one yet since it just came on the market this morning, but it looks very promising and could go fast. Would you mind if we looked at it for the first time together?"

7. When you suggest to a real estate agent that one particular home in a neighborhood you are considering looks pretty sleazy, he replies, "Yes, but I've heard they are planning to move, and new owners always tidy things up, so think how much that will increase the value of property here!"

Strategy: My decision would depend upon how sleazy the home looks and what my other options are. I wouldn't take as gospel the impending move story. This is a variation on stock answer number 47 to the "this looks like a messy neighborhood" objection.

8. Every time you ask your real estate agent a question while being shown a home, she answers with a question of her own.

Strategy: Here's how it goes. You ask, "Does the refrigerator stay?" The agent answers, "Is it important to you that the refrigerator stay?" It's a technique designed to get you talking and to more clearly define your real motive in asking the question. You must be persistent if you really want to know if the refrigerator stays.

9. The real estate agent showing you a home keeps writing furiously on a big pad of yellow paper, even though you aren't aware of saying anything worthy of inscribing.

Strategy: The theory is that the homebuyer needs to be accustomed to seeing the agent put things down on paper so he or she won't panic when the agent pulls out an offer-to-purchase form and starts writing.

10. Every time you offer a criticism of a home you are viewing there is about a 15-second delay before the real estate agent responds.

Strategy: Every conceivable common objection to buying a home has been identified and cataloged, along with an appropriate response. If you are dealing with a Theory M agent, the delay is to make you think that the response is not canned, which it is.

11

•••••▼•••••

At Last: You Look at Houses!

Some revolutionary changes may soon take place in how we shop for homes. It might go something like this. You learn you are being transferred to Topeka. After you finish celebrating, you put down your glass of champagne, rush to your computer and plug into Galaxy 2000, your interactive real estate network. You enter your destination, price range and other requirements, and immediately displayed before you in living color with accompanying music by the Boston Pops and narrative by Robert Redford are an array of possible properties. You punch a few more keys, issue a few verbal commands and additional information is immediately transmitted to you through your printer, which is tied in to your computer. You review it all, choose the most likely prospects, make an appointment to see them and start making travel arrangements. No matter how glitzy it may all get, however, ultimately you will still have to jump in the car, probably with an agent, and go out to inspect the merchandise.

The Perfect 10 Is a Fantasy

We now fast-forward to Topeka. You have selected a real estate agent with whom to work and have had your initial interview. As you are leaving the parking lot to look at homes with your friendly REALTOR®

(a retired U.S. Army master sergeant), she turns to you, grabs you by the shoulders, looks you straight in the eye and says, "Now look, soldier, there's one thing we need to get perfectly clear before we look at the first place. There is no such thing as a perfect house. Got that? Read my lips: No... such... thing... as... a... perfect... house."

Well, your agent may not be quite that direct, but somehow the point is likely to be made. It should be, for it's true. Even if you were to hire an architect to design the home of your dreams that incorporates every feature contained in ten years of clippings you've saved from *Good Housekeeping* and hired the best builder in town to build it for you, the day you move in you would probably discover something you wished you had done differently. At least that's the story we like to tell home-buyers who keep finding fault with everything we show them.

In both politics and homebuying we are dealing with the art of the possible, and compromise is a practical necessity. You will be ready for that challenge if you have decided ahead of time which features are negotiable and which are not. The problem is that it's a lot easier sitting around a table making notes and compiling lists than it is when you actually start looking at houses.

You Will Need a Scorecard

It will be very difficult for you to look at more than five or six homes in one day. It may be necessary to look at more, however, if you are in town for only a short period of time, but typically your agent will show you just three or four homes in a day.

There are several reasons. First, after awhile everything becomes a blur. Was it the blue house on Elm that had the beautiful spa, or was it the brown house on Maple? Which one had that great assumable FHA loan? To keep things straight, you need a scorecard and you need to take notes as you proceed. You will probably want to do that as you are looking at each house, or immediately after you finish looking at each one.

If the listing agents of the homes you visit are on the ball, each will have a flyer already prepared and available at the house. This is quite common and some are very elaborate and include photos, floor plans and even financing information. Or your real estate agent may provide you with data on each house ahead of time as well as some type of form to help you keep track of things. If none of those things happen or if you just want to organize your affairs so they make sense to you, take along a modest little school notebook with lined pages. Jot down important features and identifying characteristics about each home, including strengths and weaknesses. This will enable you to differentiate one property from another later and ask for additional information or arrange for a follow-up visit on those properties that pass your first cut.

There's another reason your REALTOR® will probably limit your initial showing to three or four homes. While people may think they know what they want in a house, they may not. Even if they do, perhaps they are unable to communicate their preferences clearly. They will, however, know absolutely and without any question, what they don't like the minute they see it and will express themselves in the most unambiguous terms (e.g., "Oh, puke. Avocado green shag carpeting.") That being the case, your REALTOR® may have to do some on-the-scene hustling and select additional showings if it becomes clear that you need to head in a slightly different direction. Thus, rather than lining up ten homes, the agent will more likely start with a few to test the waters.

Looking at Houses

After all the preliminaries, you finally get to look inside a few houses; but you may be limited as to how much actual productive snooping you can do, particularly if the homeowners are present. You can, however, learn a lot by some disciplined but discreet observation. Remember that you will make any offer subject to more detailed inspections later. Finally, there's no rule that says the whole thing can't be fun, but keep your goal clearly in mind: to select a home on which you will make an offer to purchase. Here are a few practical suggestions.

Getting There

When your real estate agent drives you to see homes, you may or may not be taken by the most direct route. If you don't know the territory, it is a good idea to scout around some on your own. You should know what is in the general surrounding area. Is there a popular drive-in restaurant several blocks away that serves as a rallying point for late-night cruisers? Is there a ballpark nearby, complete with a very efficient loudspeaker system? Are there large tracts of undeveloped land nearby?

Hi, Neighbor

You also need to check out the immediate neighborhood. What you should look for is an obvious pride of ownership. Folks out puttering in their yards with their rosebushes is a very good sign. Pickup trucks on blocks is a very bad sign. Homes in a particular area don't need to be expensive, but they do need to be neat and well maintained.

I putter in my yard a lot. Here's what I notice when a nearby home comes on the market. As potential buyers drive by, they eyeball the neighborhood as carefully as they eyeball the home that's for sale. When the National Association of REALTORS® did a survey a few years back, they asked buyers why they chose the home they did. Price was mentioned most frequently, which makes sense, but close behind was neighborhood.

Here's another neighborly suggestion. If you get serious about a home, take some time to walk around the neighborhood and knock on doors. Introduce yourself as a prospective neighbor and ask how they like living there. There are some commonsense precautions, such as beat a hasty retreat if, after you ring the doorbell, you see someone peering from a window with an assault rifle at the ready.

● ●

We Would Love To Have You As a Neighbor, But . . .

You often hear stories about the great real estate deal that got away. Occasionally you hear one about the missed opportunity that turned out to be a blessing. A friend of mine tells the following story that clearly illustrates the benefits of checking with the folks who know the neighborhood best, those who live there.

"When I was looking for a house, I made an offer on a home in what appeared to be a very nice neighborhood. I noticed that the next-door neighbor seemed to be taking a great deal more interest in my purchase than would normally be the case. The first time I met her she asked if I would be getting a professional to inspect the home. I said I was. Each time I talked to her she asked about the inspection and seemed to be bursting at the seams to tell me something. Finally she said she could remain silent no longer and chronicled a series of previous disasters with the home that she had witnessed, including some rather severe water problems caused by drainage from the beautiful nearby hills. If it had not been for her, I would have made a very unwise purchase."

● ●

View from the Outside

As you approach a house, you can learn a great deal about it by some methodical observations. Here are a few items you should be checking out:

The Yard.   If you are looking at an older home, the chances are good that the occupants have done what most of us do—overplant. Even new-home developers frequently overplant because they have to plant a lot of small trees and shrubs to make the new home look impressive. The problem is that in ten years or so it gets out of hand. Fortunately, this is a problem you can remedy. You would be amazed what a transformation can take place by letting a little air and sunlight in. Plants growing in contact with the house and trees that overhang roofs are particular problems. Ivy up the side of a wall may remind you of your alma mater, but you don't want it on your home—particularly if the home has a wood exterior.

The Roof.   If you've never had a leaky roof, you cannot fully appreciate what an ugly situation it can be. First, when do you become aware that your roof leaks? When it's pouring rain, of course. Locating a professional roofer to answer an emergency call during a downpour is chancy at best, and crawling around a dark attic and slippery roof trying to find and plug a leak yourself is not fun.

The most common types of roofing material are asphalt shingle, wood shake and tile, with several variations on each. No matter the type, look for signs of discoloration, damage and recently replaced surfaces. If it's a flat roof, pay particular attention, for they seem to develop difficulties more frequently than the others. Wood-shake roofs look nice, but the quality of the wood has decreased markedly in the past few years. In addition, insurance companies always charge you a higher premium for a home with a wood roof for a simple reason: it burns.

Underhouse

In some parts of the country it is common to build a home on a concrete slab, in which case you have no underhouse to worry about. In others there is some type of crawl space beneath the structure, where all sorts of unpleasant things can develop. As a minimum, ask where the access to the underhouse is located. If possible, stick your head in and shine a flashlight around. If you hear the rustling of little feet, you may have a wildlife problem. One reason inspectors get a decent wage is that they have to grovel around on their stomachs in dark places, so let them earn their money.

● ●

My, What a Pleasant Sound

Our current home is constructed on a continuous concrete foundation on a sloping lot. That means there is a large area under the house. I didn't bother to look there before we bought the home. One evening we were in the living room sitting by a cozy fire when I heard what sounded like a gurgling brook. At first I thought it was the seasonal stream at the rear of our property, but on closer inspection it seemed to be coming out of the register on the floor that delivered heat to the house. I scouted around and found the trapdoor that led to the underhouse. When I shined my flashlight down, I saw my reflection in a very large body of water. After a few days of panic trying to find the source of our unwanted lake, we discovered that an underground water pipe to the house had come loose and was leaking, which caused the water to accumulate at the exact point under the house where the main heating duct connects to the heater. It must have been leaking for a long time to have resulted in that much water. It was a fairly simple problem to correct but did require us to replace a rusted duct. A simple inspection would have revealed this problem.

● ●

Basements

These are defined as spaces in a home that are below the exterior grade. The words *below ground* are often synonymous with *water problems.* Look for evidence of leaking walls. If there are many large items stored in the basement, make sure your inspector looks behind them to see if they are hiding large water stains.

In the House

Take a look at the ceiling to see if there are any water stains. Inhale deeply to see if there is evidence of a pungent pet who in an emergency has used the den rug as his potty. Check out the kitchen and bathrooms closely, for these rooms get a lot of use, and with use come problems. It isn't always a sure sign, but it's encouraging if everything is neat, tidy and apparently well cared for.

Providing Feedback

After each showing, or after seeing all the houses scheduled for that day, it's probable that your agent will ask for formal feedback. You will be asked questions such as "Are we on the right track?", "Which house came the closest to meeting your needs?", "Is there one on which you want more detailed information?" and "Did you see one you think you might like to make an offer on?" This last question is intended to ensure that an element of reality is occasionally introduced to remind you that the purpose of the entire exercise is to find a home for you to buy.

If, after going out on several house-hunting expeditions, you haven't made an offer to purchase, your REALTOR® may start to get a little nervous. As a conscientious professional who knows that her time is valuable, she has done a lot of preparatory work and has selected what she believes are the best homes on the market in your price range to show you. After she's given it her best shot and you don't make an offer, one of several possibilities exist.

The first possibility is that she has failed to grasp what you really want in a home. If that's the case, she'll keep showing, probing and asking questions until she gets it right. The second is that you know what you want but are determined to see all reasonable possibilities before you make a decision. (There's a third possibility, that you don't know what you want and wouldn't recognize it if it fell on you, but we'll discount that one for now.)

Presuming you are confident enough in your own judgment to act when you need to, looking at a lot of homes is certainly not an unrealistic expectation. Here's an example.

●●●

This Is You . . . Trust Me

Dave Liniger is the cofounder and chairman of the board of RE/MAX International, one of the most successful, vigorous real estate franchise operations in North America. RE/MAX is the continent's leading 100 percent franchise operation. That means that a RE/MAX agent gets all of the commission, as opposed to splitting it with the broker. However, the agent pays for all business and personal expenses plus a substantial monthly fee to the office, which means that only top producers are typically attracted to RE/MAX.

When Liniger decided he wanted to buy a ranch in California, he naturally worked with a RE/MAX agent. As he relates in his book *Maximums* (RE/MAX International Inc. 1991), the agent showed him only one property. He assured Liniger that he had previewed all the other possibilities and in the interest of efficient time management for both of them, had eliminated each. Liniger said he appreciated that, but since this was the first ranch he had ever purchased, and for his own peace of mind, he wanted to see 15 or 20 possibilities—i.e., everything available in his price range. Dave Liniger knows real estate. If he insists on reviewing all the prospects before deciding, then that seems to be a pretty good strategy for the rest of us.

●●●

While careful consideration and studied deliberation are admirable traits for homebuyers, when bells and whistles go off and your gut feeling tells you that you've found your heart's desire, you need to be ready to act. That means making a formal offer to purchase subject to a series of very careful formal inspections, just to make certain that your gut feeling isn't merely a case of indigestion.

▼

Red Flag Checklist and Survival Strategies

1. You are relocating to a new city and have flown in on a house-hunting visit. As you are looking at homes with the real estate agent, you are impressed that you haven't seen any really bad neighborhoods or blighted areas.

Strategy: It would be wise to rent a car and tour the city on your own, just to become familiar with it. Even if it means a slight detour, a real estate agent will typically not choose to motor you by the city dump or local graffiti exhibit. It isn't a bad idea to check before you go on your own little expedition to see if there are certain combat zones you should avoid.

2. You've listed "great view" as a requirement for the home in the hills you are searching for. An agent tells you he knows of one with a "peek-a-boo" view.

Strategy: That's real estate talk meaning you have a view when the wind is blowing sufficiently hard to move away the two towering redwoods located in front of your picture window. If a great view is a must, you will have to keep looking or get out the chain saw.

3. When asked about a particular feature in a house, your mate's typical reaction during a house-hunting expedition is, "I don't really care. If you like it, it's fine with me."

Strategy: It would be highly desirable if you could coax your recalcitrant mate into participating more enthusiastically in the decision-making process. The more input you have, the better the chance that you will make a decision both of you can be happy with a few years down the line.

4. One home you have seen is listed as an "estate sale."

Strategy: This could mean it may take longer to negotiate, since attorneys and judges are sometimes involved. Perhaps there has been a formal appraisal to independently establish value. You can sometimes get a good deal on one of these homes if there are anxious heirs.

5. A home you are scheduled to look at has what is described as "electric ceiling heat."

Strategy: This was popular for a very short time several years ago in a few parts of the country. The heating cables are located (buried) in the ceiling itself. When something goes wrong, you have to tear into the ceiling. Another problem is that heat rises, so it is difficult to get the temperature in a room even. Electric ceiling heat didn't remain a popular feature for long. Avoid it if possible.

6. The home you are considering is in a residential area within the city limits and across the street from a health club and a large tract of undeveloped land.

Strategy: While it would be convenient to have a health club nearby, its presence should signal a warning sign about the undeveloped land. It's possible that the land is zoned for commercial or multifamily residential use (duplexes, apartment houses, etc.). You might even be looking at a future minimall on the land. Check on the zoning.

7. As a real estate agent is showing you a home, your mate exclaims, "Oh look, this would be a perfect spot for little Eldred's bunk bed, and he could put the case with his pet tarantula collection in the corner."

Strategy: In the business, this is known as a buying signal. If you start placing furniture, it's a pretty good sign you are mentally moving into the house. This is no big problem, but a more restrained enthusiasm while in the presence of sellers and/or real estate agents is the recommended strategy.

8. In looking over a flyer for a home that is for sale, you notice the phrase "sump pump in basement in good working order." You don't know what function a sump pump performs.

Strategy: A sump is a pit or reservoir constructed to hold water as it accumulates. The sump pump discharges it. When mentioned in connection with a basement, it will typically mean there are water problems.

9. You are considering a home that's about 50 years old. It has been completely remodeled. However, it has the original oil furnace, which is in the basement.

Strategy: One of the most frequent locations of asbestos is the insulation for pipes associated with old oil or coal furnaces. Problems can occur if the asbestos insulation starts to deteriorate and fibers are released in the air. It can be very costly to remove asbestos insulation.

10. *You've located a nice little home that fits your budget, but it's located in a neighborhood that also contains several duplex rental units.*

Strategy: Here's the problem. Rental units typically aren't as well maintained as owner-occupied homes. Tenants come and go frequently. Landlords change. If there are other options, I would consider them seriously.

12

Inspection in Depth

During the cold war there was an air defense strategy for North America known as defense in depth. It basically was designed to identify and counter potential threats as early as possible and by as many means as possible. We can apply the same concept to inspecting homes—inspection in depth. Your goal is to have as many formal and informal inspections as practical on any home for which you make an offer.

Inspection: Your Strategy

What follows is an overview of the inspection-in-depth strategy. The process actually started when you were looking at homes with your REALTOR®. Since you were an observant, note-taking participant at that time, you will be well prepared for what is to follow.

Contingencies

When you make your formal offer to purchase, it should be subject to a number of contingencies. "Subject to" simply means that certain things must happen before your offer is binding. For example, you should tender your offer subject to obtaining financing that is acceptable to you.

I strongly recommend that you make your offer subject to the following contingencies:

- *Your personal formal inspection.* This just means that you will return to the house and take a closer look without a scowling homeowner peering over your shoulder. If it's a new home or is not occupied, you will have the freedom to do your poking in private, perhaps anytime you wish.

- *A formal inspection.* This inspection must be conducted by a professional inspector who is selected and paid for by you, with the results approved by you. This is a good idea even if it's a new home.

- *A final walk-through inspection.* This inspection will be done by you and/or your inspector after the sellers have vacated the premises and a day or so prior to closing (the day you fork over that humongous final check and get the deed to the property). Even if the home is vacant when you look at it the first time, or if it's a new home, I still recommend a final walk-through just prior to closing.

Self-Inspections

There is a practical legal reason why you should personally inspect a home very carefully before you buy it. If there is an obvious problem that is readily apparent to anyone with even minimal powers of observation, you probably won't be able to claim later that you were deceived. I say "probably" because there is a very complex legal theory that applies in such situations. It's called "who knows?" How things will turn out in a lawsuit depends upon the specific situation and the comparative skills of the competing attorneys. Your objective is to avoid any of these future unpleasantries.

You may be limited as to how much probing you can do personally, but do as much as is reasonably possible. You can certainly make valuable visual observations without getting under the house yourself and consorting with the spider population.

What To Inspect

There is a story from the World War II era told about a young second lieutenant who was eager to establish his authority and bedazzle the troops with his brand-new shiny gold bars. One morning as he was inspecting the mess hall, he walked up to a large pot with liquid in it and tasted its contents. He immediately spit it out and screamed at the mess sergeant, "You call this soup?" "No, sir," replied the mess sergeant calmly, "We call that dishwater."

While it's clear that you must know what you are inspecting to make a valid judgment, it is equally important that you know what items in a house need to be inspected. We can get a lot of help in that task by taking a look at the subject of mandatory seller disclosure.

Disclosure: Your Ally

The majority of states now have mandatory seller property disclosure. This simply means that the seller is required to fill out a very comprehensive form about the property. The form is quite complete and asks a lot of very pointed questions.

• •

For Me? What a Nice Surprise!

I traveled to California a few years ago to sell my mother's house so that I could settle her estate. At that time I was actively selling real estate in Oregon, where there then were no mandatory seller disclosure requirements. I selected a REALTOR® to list the home. Imagine my surprise when she handed me a lengthy, very legal-looking property disclosure form and gently said, "You will need to fill this out. I'm not allowed to help you. Don't forget to sign it and date it." I quickly concluded that I needed to start checking things out very carefully before I signed the form.

• •

Included below are a number of the pertinent disclosure items required by the California Civil Code. It will be instructive for you to take a few minutes to read them over. The California code will give you a good overview of the items you and your inspector should be looking at and will pinpoint several potential problem areas. As you read the material, please remember that this excerpt doesn't contain the entire provisions of the code and is included for illustrative purposes only.

Real Estate Transfer Disclosure Statement
The following are excerpts from the California Civil Code.
***
II
Seller's Information
The Seller discloses the following information with the knowledge that even though this is not a warranty, prospective Buyers may rely on this information in deciding whether and on what terms to purchase the subject property. . . .

THE FOLLOWING ARE REPRESENTATIONS MADE BY THE SELLER(S) AND ARE NOT REPRESENTATIONS OF THE AGENT(S), IF ANY. THIS INFORMATION IS A DISCLOSURE AND IS NOT IN-TENDED TO BE PART OF ANY CONTRACT BETWEEN THE BUYER AND SELLER. . . .

A. The subject property has the items checked below:

__Range	__Oven
__Microwave	__Dishwasher
__Trash compactor	__Garbage disposal
__Washer/Dryer hookups	__Window screens
__Rain gutters	__Burglar alarms
__Smoke detector(s)	__Fire alarm
__TV antenna	__Satellite dish
__Intercom	__Central heating
__Central air	__Evaporator cooler
__Wall/Window air conditioner	__Sprinklers
__Public sewer	__Septic tank
__Sump pump	__Water softener
__Patio/Decking	__Built-in barbecue
__Gazebo	__Security gate(s)
__Sauna	__Garage door opener
__Spa __Hot tub	__Number remote
__Pool	__Garage: __Attached
__Pool/Spa heater:	__Not attached __Carport
__Gas __Solar __Electric	__Water heater:
__Water supply:	__Gas __Electric
__City __Well	Fireplace(s):__
__Other	Gas starter__
Exhaust fan(s)__	220 Volt wiring__

Roof(s): Type:___ Age: ___ (approx.)
Other: _____
    Are there, to the best of your (Seller's) knowledge, any of the above
that are not in operating condition? ___Yes ___ No
    If yes, then describe. (Attach additional sheets if necessary.) _____

B. Are you (Seller) aware of any significant defects/malfunctions in any
   of the following? ____Yes ____ No If yes, check appropriate space(s)
   below.

__Interior walls	__Ceilings
__Floors	__Exterior walls
__Insulation	__Roof(s)
__Windows	__Doors
__Foundation	__Slab(s)
__Driveways	__Sidewalks
__Walls/Fences	__Electrical systems
__Plumbing/Sewer/Septics	

   Other structural components (Describe.) _____
_____
_____

    If any of the above is checked, explain. (Attach additional sheets if
necessary.) _____
_____
_____

C. Are you (Seller) aware of any of the following:
   1. Substances, materials or products which may be an environ-
      mental hazard such as, but not limited to, asbestos, formalde-
      hyde, radon gas, lead-based paint, fuel or chemical storage tanks,
      and contaminated soil or water on the subject property.
                                              ____Yes ____No
   2. Features of the property shared in common with adjoining land-
      owners, such as walls, fences and driveways, whose use or re-
      sponsibility for maintenance may have an effect on subject
      property. ____Yes ____No
   3. Any encroachments, easements or similar matters that may affect
      your interest in the subject property. ____Yes ____No
   4. Room additions, structural modifications or other alterations or
      repairs made without necessary permits. ____Yes ____No
   5. Room additions, structural modifications or other alterations or
      repairs not in compliance with building codes.
                                              ____Yes ____No

6. Landfill (compacted or otherwise) on the property or any portion thereof. ____Yes ____No
7. Any settling from any cause, or slippage, sliding or other soil problems. ____Yes ____No
8. Flooding, drainage or grading problems. ____Yes ____No
9. Major damage to the property or any of the structures from fire, earthquake, floods or landslides. ____Yes ____No
10. Any zoning violations, nonconforming uses, violations of "setback" requirements. ____Yes ____No
11. Neighborhood noise problems or nuisances. ____Yes ____No
12. CC&Rs or other deed restrictions or obligations. ____Yes ____No
13. Homeowners' Association which has any authority over the subject property. ____Yes ____No
14. Any "common area" (facilities such as pools, tennis courts, walkways or other areas co-owned in undivided interest with others). ____Yes ____No
15. Any notices of abatement or citations against the property. ____Yes ____No
16. Any lawsuits against the Seller threatening to or affecting this real property. ____Yes ____No

Seller certifies that the information herein is true and correct to the best of Seller's knowledge as of the date signed by Seller.

Seller: _____   Date: _____
Seller: _____   Date: _____

III
Agent's Inspection Disclosure

(To be completed only if the Seller is represented by an agent in this transaction)

THE UNDERSIGNED, BASED ON THE ABOVE INQUIRY OF THE SELLER(S) AS TO THE CONDITION OF THE PROPERTY AND BASED ON A REASONABLY COMPETENT AND DILIGENT VISUAL INSPECTION OF THE ACCESSIBLE AREAS OF THE PROPERTY IN CONJUNCTION WITH THAT INQUIRY, STATES THE FOLLOWING:

_____
_____
_____
_____

Agent (Broker Representing Seller): _____

By: _____ Date: _____
(Associate Licensee or Broker/Signature)

***
V
BUYER(S) AND SELLER(S) MAY WISH TO OBTAIN PROFESSIONAL
ADVICE AND/OR INSPECTIONS OF THE PROPERTY AND TO PRO-
VIDE FOR APPROPRIATE PROVISIONS IN A CONTRACT BETWEEN
BUYER AND SELLER(S) WITH RESPECT TO ANY ADVICE/INSPEC-
TIONS/DEFECTS.
***
A REAL ESTATE BROKER IS QUALIFIED TO ADVISE ON REAL
ESTATE. IF YOU DESIRE LEGAL ADVICE, CONSULT YOUR AT-
TORNEY.

Disclosure and Inspection: The Rest of the Story

There are several additional points to make about disclosure.

- Getting a complete seller disclosure is important, but it doesn't
  mean that you shouldn't conduct inspections of your own. Furthermore, not all states have seller disclosure requirements. Even in
  those states, however, many real estate brokers insist upon them
  before they will list a home. As a buyer, no matter what the rules
  are where you live, you can and should insist upon a seller disclosure form. In addition to the protection it provides, it can serve as
  a checklist for your inspections. Check with your REALTOR® to see
  what's available locally. If there's something you want to know
  about that's not on the form, ask that it be added.

- Even among states that require disclosure, the specific details can
  differ substantially. For example, the environmental disclosure requirements are greater in some states than others. There also are
  differing policies regarding disclosure of such things as crimes that
  have been committed in the property or whether someone has died
  from a communicable disease.

- Note these very important words in the introductory paragraph of
  California's statement: "It is not a warranty of any kind by the
  seller(s) or any agent(s) representing any principal(s) in this transaction, and is not a substitute for any inspections or warranties the

principal(s) may wish to obtain." One of the dangers of requiring a formal written disclosure by sellers is that buyers may tend to be lulled into a false sense of security and therefore may be less vigilant in arranging for other inspections.

- Remember that any disclosure is only as trustworthy as the person making it. While most sellers will be honest, you can't count on it. You must double-check everything. If the seller is not honest and a problem develops later, you may have a strong case for misrepresentation; but if the seller is long gone into the sunset, it may not do you much good.

- You will notice that the real estate agent who listed the property is not making the basic disclosures. The sellers are on their own. The listing agent is required to do a "reasonably competent and diligent visual inspection of the accessible areas of the property. . . ." While other states have different rules, that is a fairly standard concept. What may differ from state to state or from judge to judge is the definition of the term *material facts,* which must be disclosed to buyers.

- California's admonition to get your real estate advice from brokers and your legal advice from attorneys is important. Unfortunately, there are a few real estate agents who are simply not wired to say, "I don't know," and some who feel more of a need to impress than to inform. Please refer to strategy #2 of "Your Lucky 13 Homebuying Survival Strategies" from Chapter 1.

Hot Disclosure and Inspection Topics

At one time the standard termite inspection was about all we needed to be concerned with when buying a home. Now more and more threats to our health and domestic tranquility seem to surface each year, so rounding up the usual suspects takes longer these days.

Pest and Dry Rot

Termites aren't the only little critters we need to be worry about. For example, when we moved to the Pacific Northwest we found out there is an industrious little ant whose favorite meal is wood. It's called, appropriately enough, the carpenter ant. If you have any type of financing, the lending institution will insist upon a thorough pest and dry-rot report. Dry rot is caused by a variety of factors, including excess moisture and inadequate ventilation.

Radon

When I was in air force basic training, we went through a gas mask drill. There was one quick-acting, deadly nerve gas, we were told, that you couldn't see, smell or taste and for which there was no known defense—which caused some of us to wonder why we were bothering with the gas mask drill. Radon has some of those same characteristics, but it is detectable, is not as deadly or quick-acting and there are effective defensive measures.

Radon is an odorless, colorless gas that is produced by decaying radioactive minerals found in the ground. Problems occur when the gas is trapped in enclosures, such as houses. In high enough doses, radon can cause cancer.

The first step is to require that your potential home be tested for radon. Even if the owner has declared that there are no radon problems, you still should get a test, unless one has been done recently by a reputable company. Whether the seller pays or you pay is a matter of negotiation. The radon test is not incredibly expensive, since testing is a growth industry and many companies have stepped in to fill the need. Some home inspectors do radon testing as a part of their inspections. If dangerous radon levels are detected, they can be reduced by improving ventilation, which may entail the installment of fans. That can get expensive.

Asbestos

Asbestos is a mineral fiber that is fire resistant and not easily destroyed. It has been used in a variety of household products, such as floor tile, roofing materials, ceilings and pipe insulation. The problem is that if the fibers become airborne and are inhaled, they can cause lung and stomach cancer. There is debate about how serious a threat asbestos really is for the ordinary home dweller. But no one debates the fact that it is wise to have an inspection to determine whether or not asbestos is present.

Houses that are over 40 years old are the most likely to have asbestos. Not all standard inspections cover asbestos, but make sure yours does.

Lead Poisoning

An excess of lead in the body can cause serious health problems, particularly for young children. Two of the most common household sources are lead-based paint and drinking water contaminated by lead pipes. Federal legislation now requires sellers and real estate agents to mention the hazards of lead-based paint if the property was built prior to 1978, but you need to have your inspector check out any property you are considering. Older homes with peeling paint that might be a temptation for young children to put in their mouths is probably the most dangerous of the lead-poisoning perils. Testing is also necessary to uncover water problems.

Urea Formaldehyde Insulation

This is an insulation material that is pumped into wall openings as a foam. It is an effective insulator, but it was found to cause serious illness when improperly installed, which unfortunately happened frequently.

For a time urea formaldehyde insulation was banned in several states. Your best bet is to avoid a home where this insulation has been used, since it got such a bad name that many future purchasers will reject it.

Buried Gas Tanks

These are quite common on rural property and can pose a monumental problem. Don't even consider a property with buried tanks, and make certain you determine conclusively whether or not they are present, since they will not be visible from the surface. Buying a home near an old service-station site is also extremely unwise, since underground leaching can occur.

Flooding

There are about 20,000 communities nationwide that have been designated by HUD as being within flood hazard areas. These are identified on what are known as flood-hazard maps or flood-insurance-rate maps. These maps are widely available, since lending institutions refer to them constantly. Flood insurance provided by private companies and subsidized by the federal government is available, but it is preferable to avoid flood hazard areas altogether if that's practical. Even if the property isn't in a floodplain, it could have a problem if it's near large drainage canals or is on the downside of a hill or a mountain.

Hiring an Inspector

Unfortunately, there isn't as much regulation of inspectors as there is with many other professions related to real estate. You therefore should do some serious checking before you hire an inspector. Here are some suggestions on selecting and working with an inspector:

- *Get recommendations from people you trust.* For example, I know a young couple who made offers on two homes before they finally purchased one. In each instance they made their offers contingent upon a satisfactory inspection, and each time their inspector discovered problems that caused them to back off. They said their inspector was a real nitpicker, but that's an admirable trait for inspectors. It may not be wise to ask your real estate agent for a recommendation for an inspector. You want an inspector who knows you are the boss and that you want everything that is important to be pointed out to you.

- *Never hire an inspector who also does repair work.* They invariably seem to discover problems in which they specialize in repairing. There's an obvious conflict of interests here.

- *Look for an inspector with a professional affiliation.* This typically means that the inspector has agreed to abide by a code of ethics and has engaged in professional education. Two of the most prominent of the national professional organizations are (1) The National Institute of Building Inspectors (NIBI) and (2) the American Society of Home Inspectors (ASHI).

- *Insist that your inspector have what is called errors and omissions insurance.* This insurance protects the inspector, and indirectly the buyer, in the event that something is missed in the inspection and it later becomes a big problem. Many inspectors do not have this insurance.

- *Ask to accompany the inspector on the formal inspection.* That shouldn't pose a problem with the inspector, and it will be very instructive for you. Maintain a low profile and let the inspector do the job, but don't be afraid to ask questions. Don't panic when the inspector finds problems. That's the purpose of the whole exercise, and remember that no house is perfect.

- *Insist upon a formal, written report and that there be no restrictions regarding to whom you may show it.* Ask to see a blank copy before the inspection so you know what will and will not be covered. If there is something you want checked out that is not part of the normal menu, it will cost you extra. Find out how much extra.

Red Flag Checklist and Survival Strategies

1. *The home you've decided to make an offer on is in a nice rural location. The current owners have been there only nine months but have decided to move to another home in the local area.*

Strategy: This may be a sign that there is something wrong with the property or the neighborhood that is causing an unexpected move. Folks don't usually relocate that soon.

2. *The inspector you want to hire has no formal background in building but was once an insurance agent.*

Strategy: I have found that some of the best inspectors are those who have had actual construction training and experience. I would go with that if at all possible.

3.   *When you ask an inspector for references from former clients, he tells you that he is just getting started in this business but can give you references from his previous profession.*

Strategy: Unless his previous profession was that of a structural engineer, I would go with an inspector with actual recent experience who can furnish references.

4.   *You notice that the ceilings in your prospective home have a distinct pebble appearance.*

Strategy: This was a common use of asbestos. It's no problem as long as it doesn't get disturbed. If the home is older, the probability of problems is increased.

5.   *When you step on the bathroom floor in a house you are considering, you notice a spongy feeling.*

Strategy: Bathrooms are notorious for developing water problems. The most common problem is caused by water that has seeped under floor coverings and has resulted in damage to the wood. Check all baths, and have your inspector do the same. Step heavily, but don't stomp.

6.   *You get an evasive answer when you ask about utility costs in a home you are previewing.*

Strategy: All homeowners have copies of their utility bills. Ask to see a representative sampling. Utility costs can be a substantial expense in home ownership, particularly with older homes in locations that have harsh weather.

7.   *High-voltage power lines are located on the rear portion of a 20-acre country parcel you are considering. They are a substantial distance from the site on which you would build your house.*

Strategy: Do electromagnetic fields around high-voltage power lines pose a health threat? One study suggests a link between exposure to high-voltage power lines and childhood leukemia. The federal Environmental Protection Agency says more research is needed. No matter what the truth is, their presence will likely have an adverse impact on the value of the land, since many people are aware of the controversy. Avoid the problem.

8. A homeowner is unable to tell you where the main water cutoff valve to the house is located.

Strategy: You must have your inspector find out where the cutoff valve is and try it out. They are sometimes buried in long-forgotten locations and are rusted solid. A broken pipe inside the house would prove disastrous if you couldn't shut off the water.

9. You run the faucet in the kitchen of a house and simultaneously turn on a faucet in the bathroom. There is a perceptible drop in volume.

Strategy: Plumbers tell me that can mean that pipes are corroded and aren't permitting sufficient volume. It would probably be a good idea to have a plumber check out the system.

10. A homeowner proudly tells you that he built the beautiful addition to his home.

Strategy: Handy homeowners sometimes fail to get proper building permits and build additions that are in violation of current building codes. That could mean safety problems. Have your inspector investigate.

13

•••••▼•••••

Offers: Where the Rubber Meets the Road

When you sign an offer to purchase, you set in motion a series of events that, assuming everything goes right, will result in your becoming a happy homeowner. The offer to purchase is called by different names in different parts of the country; the person writing it up may be a real estate agent or an attorney (or even you); and the procedures may vary slightly. The end result, however, is intended to be the same. The process deserves your very, very thoughtful attention.

Making the Offer: Serious Stuff

The single most important thing to keep in mind about making an offer to purchase is that you are signing a document that can result in your being committed to a legally binding contract. You aren't just sending up a trial balloon to see what the seller will actually take for the property.

I like the way the California Association of REALTORS® put it in their recently revised "Real Estate Purchase Contract and Receipt for Deposit." At the top of the form in block capital letters, just under the title, is this statement: "THIS IS MORE THAN A RECEIPT FOR MONEY. IT IS INTENDED TO BE A LEGALLY BINDING CONTRACT. READ IT CAREFULLY."

If you make the offer, the seller accepts it and you are notified of that acceptance, you have probably entered into an enforceable agreement. Before getting into the details of your offer, we need to make the following important points:

- *See a lawyer.* Now you really do need to get legal advice, assuming you have not already. In most states real estate licensees are permitted to prepare offers to purchase, although there has been an ongoing turf war between the legal profession and the real estate profession as to whether or not that is the practice of law and should therefore be the proper domain of attorneys. Most states permit real estate practitioners to write up this document, which becomes a contract, but they are supposed to merely fill in the blanks of the form as you direct them, without offering advice. Does it work that way in practice? Well, maybe not always. The best course of action is to have your attorney draft your offer. The next best course is to have a real estate agent fill out your offer subject to your attorney's approval. I advise this course of action whether you are represented by a buyer's broker or not.

- *Understand that variety rules.* There are only a few states that have a mandatory form that must be used as an offer to purchase. In most states there are several forms from which to choose, and they can differ significantly. Even in those states with standardized forms, the forms can be altered by mutual agreement of the parties to delete some provisions and include others. As offer-to-purchase agreements have evolved, it is generally acknowledged that they have been written to favor sellers. That is changing somewhat, as evidenced by mandatory property and agency disclosure laws, but many of these changes are really designed to protect the real estate licensees.

- *Put it in writing.* You will do a lot of talking before you actually write up an offer to purchase. The problem with talk is that people filter everything through their own frame of reference and naturally tend to interpret things to their own advantage. Memories become very selective when disputes arise. Unless it is written into the contract, you may have a very difficult time asserting later that you were misled. If something is important to you, get it in writing.

- *Know whose court the ball is in.* The whole business of offers and counteroffers is a little bit like a game of tennis. You write up an offer and submit it to the sellers and the ball is in their court. They make a counteroffer and the ball is back in your court. You counter their counter and you've sent the ball back.

  There are several important things you should know about this process. First, the most important thing is that you are on your way to entering into a legal contract. Second, if you make an offer that the seller counters, it is actually a rejection and lets you off the hook if you want to be off the hook. Third, if you are represented by an agent in the transaction, delivery of news to your agent will likely be construed as delivery to you. As you are working with your attorney, it would be good to get briefed occasionally as to where the ball is and who has what responsibility.

Your Offer: The Nitty-Gritty

Despite the wide variety in forms and procedures, offers to purchase contain many of the same features.

Offering Price

One feature is offering price. How much should you offer? You already know the answer: "It depends." To arrive at a decision, ask yourself the following questions:

How Much Can I Afford?　Let's say the asking price of a home is $135,000; but based upon the cash you have for a down payment and closing costs and the amount of the loan your lender has prequalified you for, $125,000 is your absolute maximum. Unless you can come up with additional funds (and your lender approves), your decision is made for you. Your top offer will be $125,000.

Is It a Buyer's or Seller's Market?　If there are a lot of homes on the market and qualified buyers are scarce, you have a buyer's market. In this case sellers tend to be much more agreeable to accepting less for their homes than they are asking and to agree to other concessions. If there are several anxious, qualified buyers and a limited supply of homes for sale, it is a seller's market. Home prices inflate rapidly, and homeowners aren't likely to want to lower their prices much, if at all. In red-hot markets, it isn't uncommon to have several offers on the same property and to get offers above the asking price. I hope you don't have to buy in that kind of market.

How Motivated Are the Sellers?   Whether the market is hot, cold or tepid, you often find very motivated sellers who are anxious to deal and depart. People who must sell to relocate for another job are generally very cooperative. Couples who are divorcing may not agree on much else, but they will often wish to liquidate the homestead quickly in the interest of dividing the assets and splitting. Empty nesters headed for milder climates may be very easy to work with. Your challenge is to find out how motivated the sellers are. Ask the real estate agent why they are selling. Also ask how long the home has been on the market. Unless you have a buyer's agent, remember that all the real estate licensees will be technically representing the seller, so you may have to read between the lines of the answer. On the other hand, they may flat-out tell you.

How Much Is the Property Worth?   One of the advantages of having looked at a lot of homes is that you will rapidly become well informed as to comparative values and should be able to recognize an overpriced property when you see it. Furthermore, you will have some protection in the lending process, since your lender will require a formal appraisal to support the loan, and you will have made your offer subject to the property qualifying for a certain mortgage amount. Be aware, however, that the lender is only interested in ensuring adequate security for the loan. If you wish to kick in another ten thousand or so to make the purchase, that's your business.

If you are working in a seller-agency relationship, remember that you may not get an unbiased, objective answer if you ask the real estate broker: "How much do you think the seller will take?" That doesn't mean you shouldn't ask the question; just consider the source.

You may not even get the best answer in the world if you are represented by a buyer's broker working on a commission. There will be a strong motivation to do what is necessary to get the transaction closed, and it is fairly apparent that buyers tend to accept higher rather than lower offers. If you do have a buyer's broker, you can ask that you be given what is called a *comparative market analysis*, which is a summary of recent sales of similar homes. It's a lot like an appraisal although less formal. Brokers prepare comparative market analyses for sellers when they are deciding upon a price.

Remember that people typically ask more for a home than they expect to get. Even in a seller's market, statistics show that final sales prices, on average, are somewhat less than asking prices. In a buyer's market they can be substantially less.

How Much Do I Want the House?   Even in a buyer's market, it's not considered subversive to offer full price for a home, although others involved in the transaction will have a difficult time not gasping in shocked disbelief if you do. If you and/or your mate conclude that you absolutely must have that cute Cape Cod on Sea Gull Circle or life as you know it will lose its meaning, throw tradition to the winds and offer what the owner is asking. This assumes, of course, that you can afford the home and can obtain the necessary financing. A lifetime of regret and/or a surly spouse is not worth a few thousand dollars.

Earnest Money Deposit

The *earnest money deposit* is the cash deposit you make with your offer to show your good faith and your intention to complete the transaction. In some places it's called a binder. The real question is, "How much earnest money deposit should I give?" There is no set amount that is mandated by law anywhere; it is all negotiable.

You have two basic motivations with your earnest money deposit. First, you want to let the sellers know that you are a serious buyer. If you offer a $500 promissory note on a $300,000 home, you aren't likely to impress anyone. Okay, but if $500 isn't appropriate, what is? One to 3 percent of the offering price is sometimes quoted as a customary minimum amount, which means between $3,000 and $9,000 on the $300,000 home. Rarely does the deposit exceed 10 percent. Again, however, the exact amount is entirely up to you. Second, you don't want to get a lot of your money tied up in a deal that hasn't yet been finalized. If the worst happened, you could lose it. In addition, never permit your earnest money to be given directly to the seller. A neutral depository, such as an escrow account or a broker's clients' trust account, is the best place for your deposit; but remember that once it gets there, it normally takes the agreement of both parties to release it.

One final point. There sometimes is confusion among buyers as to what purpose the earnest money deposit serves. Some think it is extra money they have to pay to secure the deal and that the money goes to the seller as an added benefit. Any earnest money you pay is credited to you and will be used to cover your transaction costs.

What's Included in the Sale?

The basic rule is that fixtures in a home go with the property, while personal property does not unless separately bargained for.

There are a few problems that can arise. First, each party may define *fixture* differently. There's generally no question that the hot water heater, for example, is a fixture and that it stays. But how about a window air conditioner? This would probably depend on how the air conditioner was attached to the window.

Things can get even more confusing when you use terms such as *window coverings*. If the buyer thinks the term includes all drapes and curtains while the seller thinks it only includes the roll-up blinds and shades, you have the stuff from which big disputes are made. If you want the drapes and curtains to stay, state that in your offer, unless it is already crystal clear that they do stay.

Freestanding appliances, such as refrigerators, freezers, washers and dryers, are also items of frequent controversy, as are light fixtures. If the listing says the refrigerator goes with the property and the refrigerator you find when you move in isn't the one you saw when you looked at the house, you will not be happy. Real estate agents have frequently purchased disgruntled homebuyers new refrigerators in such instances, since the sellers have long since departed. You can avoid this by having each major item of personal property that goes with the property de-scribed in writing on the offer to purchase or on a separate document, including the serial number of high-ticket items such as refrigerators. On very unique items, such as fantastic antique light fixtures, do not automatically assume that they stay. I know one homeowner who was so attached to her prize rhododendron in the front yard that she dug it up and took it with her, replacing it with a container plant from the local discount store.

Your Attention, Please: Contingencies

This is essentially what you are saying when you make an offer to purchase a home: "I offer you $150,000 for your property, subject to the following contingencies. . . ." If the contingencies are not satisfied, the intent is that you can walk away from the transaction, along with your earnest money deposit. It is imperative that you know what contingencies to include, and it is equally important that the wording of them be precise. You must confer with someone well versed in drafting contingencies, preferably an attorney. Some common contingencies are as follows:

- *Financing.* Even if you have been prequalified for a specific mortgage amount, interest rates and terms can change rapidly. You want to be able to back off if you cannot get a loan at the interest rate and the terms you desire. In all instances it is wise to have the contingencies worded so that your approval is needed before a contingency is removed.

- *Property Qualification.* To get an objective assessment, the lender will have the property formally appraised. You pay for this service. Lenders use the term *loan to value,* which means that if you buy a home for $100,000 (value) and put $20,000 down, they will have loaned you 80 percent of the value of the home. That's fine if the property is appraised at $100,000. But let's say it is appraised at only $90,000. In this case their maximum 80 percent loan to value would be $72,000. Your purchase should be contingent upon the property qualifying for the loan amount you desire. If it doesn't, you can renegotiate with the seller for a different price or work with the bank for different terms.

- *Inspections.* We have already discussed inspections, but we need to reemphasize that your offer will be contingent upon your own personal inspection and other inspections that you deem appropriate, for which you will pay. One inspector may be able to do the entire job, or you may have to get a few inspectors. For example, some general inspectors are licensed to do pest and dry rot in addition to general inspections; others may not be licensed in this area. You will get some protection from the appraiser also, for if a condition turns up that looks iffy, the bank will be notified and will require that it be checked out.

- *Approval by a Third Party.* Real estate agents hate approval by a third party. They finally get you to make a written offer only to find out that they now have to get someone else's concurrence. Typically it means that your mom and dad or son or daughter or Aunt Harriet or Uncle Ludwig have to approve the property and the deal. Sometimes the third party is supplying part of the funding, so it's not an unreasonable contingency. However, it can get tricky if it becomes apparent that the third party isn't really entering into the thing in a spirit of objectivity.

   I once wrote up an offer on a home to a young bachelor with the contingency that his dad had to approve. The problem was that dad was judging the property by what he could afford, not what his son could afford.

   It is wise to get the advice of others whom you trust before you make such an important decision, but remember that in the final analysis you are the one who has to live in the property. If you include this contingency, put a short time limit on it or the sellers will probably not be receptive.

- *Selling Another Property.* I've already mentioned that if you have a home you have to sell first, you are wise to do that before you begin house hunting seriously. However, you may not have any control over the situation. If that's the case, go ahead and make your offer contingent upon selling your home, but don't expect an enthusiastic response, and make sure you have a Plan B.

Boilerplate Specials

There are standard forms and formats that are commonly used in real estate transactions, whether they are preprinted or stored in a computer. The following list includes some of the topics that are typically covered, but you are advised to discuss the entire document with your attorney.

- *Close Date.* This is the date you officially become the homeowner and money changes hands—from your hands to those of the seller. In most transactions it will take at least 60 days. If a real estate agent tells you it will take significantly less time, be very skeptical.

- *Title Insurance.* You want to know that the owner has good title to the property and that if a title dispute arises later, you are protected. Title insurance gives you this protection, but note that there are a few different options. Standard coverage is what most buyers get, but I recommend extended coverage. This costs more, but it offers important additional protection.

  It is customary in most places for the seller to pay for title insurance, but that varies and is negotiable. If you want extended coverage, you may have to pay for it. If so, shop around for rates. The buyer always pays for mortgagee title insurance, which ensures title for the lending institution.

- *Possession.* In the normal course of events, possession of the property occurs after the transaction closes, but there are times when the purchaser moves in prior to closing on a per-day rental agreement. Sellers are often amenable to this arrangement, since it means extra money in their pockets. Real estate agents, on the other hand, strongly counsel sellers to resist rental arrangements. This is because until money actually changes hands, people can become unhappy and back out. Those who move in on a temporary rental agreement in anticipation of a sale often become disgruntled when they find they haven't purchased the perfect home. If all parties are reasonable, however, it can be a convenient way of getting out of the motel and into the new home ahead of time. Be very certain that your agreement stipulates who is responsible for property hazard insurance prior to the actual closing. It could be you once you take possession.

- *Arbitration.* Many standard sales agreements now contain a feature known as mandatory arbitration. That simply means that as a buyer, you agree to submit disputes to an arbitrator rather than go to court. Discuss this matter very carefully with your attorney, since you are giving up an important right. Remember, even if it's part of the printed form, it can be deleted.

In many homebuying transactions the offer to purchase is written up in a few minutes, it is presented and accepted without delay, contingencies are satisfied with no difficulty and the buyer, seller and real estate agents all emerge at the end with smiles of satisfaction. Our goal is to ensure that you are still smiling a few years down the road.

• • ▼ •

Red Flag Checklist
and Survival Strategies

1.   You encounter a home that is priced substantially below market value.

Strategy: You may have found a nugget worth plucking. On the other hand, there are probably good reasons for the bargain price. Your challenge is to find out what they are.

2.   You locate a home that is for sale by the owner, without the services of a real estate agent. He seems very naive and uninformed on real estate matters.

Strategy: Don't let down your guard. Observe all the cautions you would if the owner were represented by a real estate broker, including having an attorney to advise you. Impressions can be very deceiving.

3.   On one of the listings in a flyer that a real estate company has prepared, you notice the phrase, "$200,000. Owner Firm."

Strategy: The word *firm* is sometimes open to interpretation. Would the owner accept $199,000 from a highly qualified buyer? Probably. Maybe even $195,000. I would only take this to mean that the seller may not be highly motivated.

4.   You tell a real estate agent that you wish to offer $175,000 on a $200,000 property. The agent responds, "I don't really believe we can submit an offer that low."

Strategy: Under most circumstances, real estate licensees are required to submit all offers to the sellers and let them make the decision. If $175,000 is what you want to offer, be persistent.

5.   In discussing an offer to purchase form with a real estate agent, you hear phrases like "that's just a standard clause in all offer to purchase forms" and "it's customary for the buyer to pay that fee."

Strategy: Because it's printed on the form doesn't make it sacred. Unless federal or state law mandates a provision, most phrases are subject to negotiation. Who pays for what is also almost always a matter of mutual agreement, despite local custom.

6.   It appears that a neighboring house is extremely close to the property line of a home you are considering.

Strategy: You may have an *encroachment,* which is an intrusion onto another person's property. The only way to uncover an encroachment is by a formal survey. Standard title insurance doesn't cover anything revealed by a survey, so you may need extended coverage. Talk to your title insurer to get terms and rates.

7.   Although a home you are considering is on a narrow, busy street, it is built quite a ways back from the front of the lot.

Strategy: This could be very deceiving. In many instances the actual lot line is considerably farther back from the street than you think. Narrow, busy streets are often widened. It is then that some homeowners find out exactly where their front property lines are located. I would insist upon a survey to locate property corners.

8.   On one listing you notice the phrase,"Sale contingent upon buyer's locating and successfully purchasing another property."

Strategy: Unless it makes little difference to you whether or when you actually buy the home in question, I would avoid this situation. It is rare, but it does happen.

9.   Because of the nature of the transaction, you have deposited $10,000 as earnest money. It looks as though it will take six months to close.

Strategy: You should insist that your money be deposited in an interest-bearing account. Propose that the interest be credited to you, although this is negotiable. Make certain the money gets in a federally insured account.

10. A farm property you are going to make an offer on has extensive equipment on the premises, such as irrigation pipes and pumps.

Strategy: Until I sold a farm, I didn't realize how expensive farm equipment is. Most of it is personal property and is usually not included in the sale. A separate personal property accounting is essential.

14

▼

Financing Your Dream

In the good old days, applying for a mortgage loan was a lot simpler than it is today. There were two basic options from which to choose: (1) the fixed-rate, fully amortizing, 30-year loan or (2) take it or leave it.

If you wanted the bank's money, you took it; and as it turned out, it was a terrific deal—for you. But as things developed it was not such a hot bargain for the lenders, so creative minds went to work and devised the smorgasbord of mortgage loan possibilities we now have. Since you will have to select one of these possibilities (unless you pay cash, of course), we need to survey the menu.

But first, a word about terminology. When you borrow money from a lending institution, you will sign a promissory note and pledge your home as collateral. The document you use to do that usually is a mortgage or trust deed, but the word *mortgage* is commonly used to describe the whole process.

Your Mortgage Loan Menu

If you have ever been in a foreign country and haven't been able to speak or read the language, you know how intimidating it is to sit down in a restaurant and try to figure out the menu. That's how most consumers feel when they are faced with the array of mortgage loan choices. It

149

will help if you are familiar with the two basic options: (1) the fixed-rate mortgage and (2) the adjustable rate mortgage. There are an almost infinite variety of each type of mortgage as well as combinations of the two, and there are other possibilities with new twists appearing each year. However, these represent the meat and potatoes of your possible selections.

Fixed-Rate, Fixed-Term, Fully Amortized Mortgages

During your prequalification interview you probably didn't spend a lot of time on specific loan possibilities, but you may have been given an overview of what was available. The fixed-rate, fixed-term mortgage that is fully paid off at the end of the loan period may have been the main topic of conversation. This type of mortgage has the following advantages:

- *Predictability.* Let's say you have a $100,000 mortgage loan at 7 percent for 30 years. Your first monthly principal and interest payment will be $665.30. So will your 360th payment. During the early years almost everything will go toward interest (tax-deductible, of course), but when you make that last payment your loan balance will be zero. The cost of living may go out of sight (what do you think a loaf of bread will cost in 30 years?), but your monthly principal and interest payment will remain the same, which means you will pay off your loan in inflated dollars. This is the mortgage loan that most borrowers prefer. I must admit I'm among them.

- *Flexibility.* The 30-year mortgage is standard, but shorter terms have become more popular in recent years. Terms of 25, 20 and 15 years are all possible. Why opt for a shorter term and higher payments? In addition to the fact that you will get a slightly lower interest rate, the major advantage is that you pay much less in total interest over the term of the loan. It's a sobering exercise to compute how much interest you will pay in 30 years on that $100,000, 7 percent loan (try $139,509).

Here's a strategy some buyers find attractive. They sign on for the 30-year loan and then make additional payments against principal when possible. Most loans permit at least some prepayment without penalty.

Be certain to coordinate with your lending institution to ensure that you are getting proper credit for your advance payments.

Adjustable Rate Mortgages (ARMs)

Everything was sailing along smoothly in the mortgage lending business while the nation's economy was on an even keel. Then came the 1980s. Double-digit inflation reared its ugly head and interest rates soared. Savings and loan institutions, which specialized in home mortgage loans, were particularly hard hit. They were stuck with a portfolio full of low-interest loans on which they were collecting fixed payments, but they had to start paying higher interest rates to savers to attract deposits. You know what resulted. Survival demanded that they come up with a system in which they shifted the interest rate fluctuation risk to the consumer. There was a lot of experimentation, but the adjustable rate mortgage (ARM) emerged as the loan that lenders could live with and consumers would accept.

The ARM's most important features are as follows:

- *Adjustability.* With an ARM, as interest rates go up, so does the rate on your loan and therefore your monthly payment. As they go down, you will generally share in the good news, although formulas for computing payments can be complex.

- *Limits on Increases.* When ARMs first appeared, it wasn't uncommon for them to have no limit on how much they could increase. Now caps are standard. This means that an ARM can increase no more than a certain percent each year, and there is a maximum increase permissible over the life of the loan. For example, there may be an annual cap of 2 percent and a life-of-loan cap of 7 percent.

- *Affordability.* Because of the risk shift, interest rates are considerably lower than they are for fixed-rate loans. That means you will be able to qualify for a larger loan. But if you get accustomed to paying a given monthly amount and that goes up, it can come as quite a shock to your family budget. Conversely, the rates can go down, but we usually have much less difficulty adjusting to a decrease.

- *Predictability.* It is important that you know exactly on what basis your ARM will be adjusted. There will be an index to which adjustments are tied and an adjustment period (which determines how often the rate may be changed). That adjustment period can be monthly (which isn't a good deal), quarterly, semiannually or annually. Most of the more popular indexes are tied to rates of U.S. Treasury securities. There will also be a margin, which represents the lender's premium for making the loan. The margin is usually 1 to 3 percentage points and typically remains constant. Lending institutions quite frequently offer teaser rates, where the initial rates are less than the agreed-upon index plus the margin. Teaser rates are temporary, so don't be overly impressed.

Other Choices

During the frantic days of the early 1980s some really unique plans emerged. A few of them are still around, although the fixed-rate mortgage and the ARM account for the overwhelming majority of current mortgage loans. Some of the other options include the following:

- *Graduated Payment Mortgages (GPMs).* GPMs were developed mainly to enable first-time homebuyers to qualify for loans during periods of high interest rates. With the GPM, the borrower pays lower monthly payments during the first few years of the loan and then larger payments at a predetermined schedule during the remainder of the term. Since the early payments aren't enough to cover the interest due on the loan, there is a feature known as negative amortization. This means that the amount of interest you don't pay is added to the principal of the loan—i.e., the more you pay, the more you owe. You can imagine the celebration at the Mortgage Bankers Association corporate headquarters when this feature was developed. If you are just beginning your trek up the income ladder and your prospects for future salary increases are solid, a GPM may be worth investigating. But you can tell I'm not enthusiastic.

- *Shared Appreciation Mortgages (SAMs).* This type of mortgage never really caught hold in the residential loan market. With a SAM, the lender makes the loan at a below-market rate for a share of the appreciated value when the property is sold or refinanced. Several sticky little details make SAMs risky. The most important is that for the lender to realize any profit, there has to be a sale or a refinance.

Thus, the lender needs a date certain by which a sale or refinance happens, neither of which may be convenient to the homeowner. SAMs are now limited almost exclusively to certain commercial transactions.

- *Growing Equity Mortgages (GEMs)*. These mortgages may have been gems for the lenders, but borrowers were less enthusiastic. The premise of a GEM is that you increase your loan payments on a predetermined schedule, thereby decreasing the term of the loan and the total amount you pay in interest. Since on most loans you can do the same thing without committing to set increases and the interest rate incentives for taking a GEM are minimal, GEMs raise the inevitable question, "Why bother?"

Assumptions

Assumable mortgages are most attractive during periods when interest rates are high. For example, if mortgage loans are running around 12 percent and you can find one you can assume for 6 percent, it is obviously a terrific opportunity.

There are literally thousands of existing loans that are assumable. For example, Federal Housing Administration (FHA) loans made before December 14, 1989, are freely assumable by owner-occupants with no mandatory qualification. Those FHA loans made after that date can be assumed by qualified owner-occupants. Department of Veterans Affairs (VA) loans issued before March 1, 1988, are also freely assumable by anyone, while those wishing to assume loans made after that date must qualify with the lender and with the VA.

A *conventional loan* is one that is made without government sponsorship, such as the FHA or VA. For many years conventional loans were freely assumable. All that changed when interest rates went berserk. It wasn't good business to permit a low-interest mortgage loan to be assumed. It was much better to require homebuyers to take out new loans at the higher interest rates. For that reason, almost all fixed-rate conventional loans now written have what are called due on sale or alienation clauses. That simply means that the loans may not be assumed by a new buyer without permission. Adjustable rate mortgages, on the other hand, are usually assumable (since there is built-in protection for the lender), but the buyer must qualify financially and must pay applicable fees.

Where does one find out about assumable loans? For listed properties, you will have to rely on real estate agents. When a listing with an attractive assumable loan comes on the market, it will be prominently featured in any promotional material. On properties that are being sold directly by the owners, you must rely only on the owners' information. However, for both listings and homes for sale by owners, it is absolutely critical to check in writing with the lending institution that holds the mortgage to verify that the loan is assumable by you and under what conditions.

Homeowners with assumable loans often have a lot of equity. That means you should figure out a way to "cash them out" or work out an arrangement where they take part of their equity in a promissory note from you that is secured by a second mortgage on the property. In a market with abundant mortgage money at low interest rates, homebuyers won't get too excited by assumable loans.

Creative Financing

The term *creative financing* covers a lot of territory and includes some tremendous opportunities, but the terrain can get a little rough. ("They had another word for creative financing in my day," says an old-timer—"Larceny.") Here are some of the possibilities:

- *Owner Financing.* There are people who own their homes free and clear. I know it sounds unbelievable, but it's true. Furthermore, when some of these folks sell, they like to act as their own bankers. That's the purest form of owner financing. If you get involved in one of these financing opportunities, understand that everything is very, very flexible. You won't be dealing with a lending institution that has rigid rules and regulations. While those institutional procedures may sometimes seem cumbersome, they do offer a considerable amount of protection. That protection will not be automatically available if you deal directly with a homeowner.

  There is one form of owner financing that merits special mention. It's called the land sales contract, and it's very popular in certain sections of the country. If you give a mortgage or trust deed to secure your promissory note, you will simultaneously get a deed to the property. But if you give a land sales contract, the title actually remains with the seller until you pay off the loan. You won't get your deed until that happens. You can see why these contracts are popular with sellers. Since the term of the land sales contract can be several years, you can appreciate how that might pose a problem. If you buy with a land sales contract, you must make certain that you do all the things that a lending institution would have done to ensure that the property is a sound investment. That means you will need a formal appraisal and formal inspections. It certainly means working with an experienced attorney.

- *Equity Sharing.* Equity sharing is simple in concept and has tremendous potential, particularly for creditworthy but cash-short homebuyers with steady incomes who are related to, or acquainted with, individuals who have some money they want to invest in real estate. The following story shows how equity sharing works.

● ●

Match Made in Heaven

Ivan Stinson is a rich almond farmer with more money in the bank than he knows what to do with. His young married son, Lem, has a good steady job and a wife with an income that slightly exceeds his. They have great long-range prospects and an impeccable credit history, but they haven't been able to save enough money for a down payment on a house. Lem hears of a program called equity sharing, where his father can contribute a large chunk of cash toward the down payment on a home that his son and daughter-in-law will help buy. The end result of the transaction is that each family will own 50 percent of the property. Lem and wife will pay Ivan 50 percent of the fair market value of the property each month in rent and 50 percent of the mortgage payment to the lender. Ivan will also pay 50 percent of the mortgage payment. He will treat the property as an investment and can write off a considerable amount on his income taxes. In addition, Lem and wife can treat their 50 percent ownership the same way as would a homeowner with the appropriate deductions. When it comes time to sell the property, they will share equally in any profit.

● ●

- Equity sharing was devised originally to help families buy property together, but it is also available to investors. If equity sharing appeals to you, find professionals who are experienced in the area to work with you. That means that you will need an attorney and your investor-partner will need an accountant.

- *Lease Options.* You don't have enough cash for a down payment and closing costs, but you do have a decent income. You locate an owner who has not been able to sell his home—perhaps it's a slow market. You agree to lease the home for a period of time with a portion, or all, of your monthly payments going toward the eventual purchase of the home if you decide to exercise your option.

    Here are some cautions. First, understand that a lease option is a legally binding contract and it must be structured to protect your interests. Second, ask yourself why the owner hasn't been able to sell the home. Is it overpriced? Is there something wrong with it? Third, be realistic as to the likelihood that you, and the property, will be able to qualify for a loan if and when you decide to buy.

All or Nothing at All

The following are some of the options that are rare, but possible:

- *All Cash.* It is very unusual for buyers to pay all cash for a property, even if they can afford it. Most people don't like to have that much of their liquid assets tied up in one investment, even if it's their own home. If you decide it's a wise course of action for you, insist upon all the safeguards that you would have with a lender, such as inspections and appraisals.

- *No Cash.* Can you buy a home with nothing down? Certainly. And you can also win the Irish Sweepstakes. Veterans Administration loans come the closest, although even they now require cash for fees. The Federal Housing Administration and the Farmers Home Administration also have programs that require little initial investment, but there are restrictions. The most likely scenario in which you might be able to swing a no-cash-down purchase would be to locate a homeowner who either owns the home free and clear or who has an assumable loan. In either instance you will need to convince the owner to take an IOU from you for the equity. If you have that type of persuasive power, I strongly advise you to immediately get into real estate sales. In very short order you won't have to worry about no-money-down deals.

Cosigners

If you are a little short of meeting a qualifying ratio, you may be able to convince a lender to relax their standards slightly if you can come up with a cosigner. It's not a step to be taken lightly, since another word for cosigner is *co-obligee*. This means your cosigner is equally responsible for the debt. Lending institutions prefer to make loans to borrowers who can qualify on their own, but they may listen if you propose a blue chip cosigner. It will also help if the cosigner happens to be on the bank's board of directors. Remember, however, if your angelic grandmother Grace agrees to cosign for you, prepare her for the rigors of submitting her financial history and having her credit checked. Lending institutions are not very sentimental.

Rich Relatives

You would think a lending institution would be delighted if your Aunt Tillie stepped forward and anted up a few grand to help you buy your home. While they are not unalterably opposed to gifts, lending institutions do have very strict rules regarding them. They prefer to lend money to someone who doesn't need a lot of help to qualify for a loan. The presumption is that if you need that much assistance, you may need additional help to pay off the mortgage. However, if Aunt Tillie insists, confer with your lender to sort it all out and do it properly.

Government Programs

Federal Housing Administration and Veterans Administration loan programs are the most well known of the government programs, but they aren't the only programs.

The Federal Housing Administration

The FHA insures loans, which makes them popular with lenders. However, they also insist that a lot of procedures be followed that don't always thrill lenders or sellers. The FHA offers a wide variety of loan programs, including fixed rates, ARMs and most of the other options. The specific details change frequently. At one time interest rates on FHA loans were regulated by the government, but that is no longer the case. There are two major advantages with FHA loans: (1) down payment requirements may be less than any conventional loan you can secure and (2) the qualification ratios are often more lenient. When you are initially investigating financing options, check with at least one local lender who makes FHA loans and get the latest information.

The Veterans Administration

The first, most obvious requirement to qualify for a VA loan is that you be an eligible veteran. To find out if you are eligible, contact your local VA representative. The most attractive feature of VA loans is that you can get a loan with very little cash up front. At one time they were truly no-down loans, but modest loan fees are now required. After you establish your eligibility with the VA, check with a local lender who makes VA loans for current interest rates and procedures. The federal government no longer regulates VA interest rates.

The Farmers Home Administration (FmHA)

If you live in or near a rural community, check with your local FmHA office to see what programs they have to offer. You don't have to be a farmer to qualify. The FmHA serves those with very modest incomes who are seeking no-frill residential housing in small rural communities. The FmHA periodically even has funds for special projects, such as buying homes that need work. Check your phone book under "U.S. Government."

State Programs

At one time or another, almost every state sponsors housing subsidy programs for low-income or first-time homebuyers. Many states also have specific programs for state veterans. The trick with state programs is to get plugged in to what's available. You will have to use your initiative to keep up-to-date by contacting state housing agencies and local lenders. In programs where bonds are sold to support the program, the money often goes fast, so you must to be ready to act.

Foreclosures

Foreclosures are not, of course, a method of financing; but quite often if a lending institution has an inventory of homes upon which they have had to foreclose, they will also arrange for attractive terms. You need to appreciate, however, how complex the foreclosure process can be. In a real estate licensing course I teach at a community college, I frequently call in local attorneys to make presentations on specialized subjects, including foreclosure. In our bucolic little state alone, it takes a Philadelphia lawyer to sort through the morass of foreclosure rules, regulations, laws and procedures. Of course, if you become very well versed in foreclosures, you may be able to locate a home at a terrific bargain and even a method of acquiring investment property. I've included a few books on foreclosure in the Bibliography. If you are intrigued by the subject, read up, but you will have to know the rules in your state. Then surround yourself with knowledgeable pros before you get serious about parting with any of your money.

• • ▼ •
Red Flag Checklist
and Survival Strategies

1. A homeowner has indicated that she will take a wraparound mortgage on her home.

Strategy: This means that the seller will take a mortgage that wraps around underlying mortgages. You will pay her, and she will pay the underlying mortgages. It's not an arrangement you want to get involved in without expert legal advice.

2. One listing your REALTOR® *shows you includes the phrase, "Owner will not sell on FHA or VA."*

Strategy: The FHA and VA have a reputation for taking a long time to process loans and for being real nitpickers. This trait may be in a buyer's interest as an owner may not think the property can pass an FHA or VA inspection.

3. A homeowner offers to let you buy his home with a substantial down payment but interest-only monthly payments with a three-year balloon.

Strategy: The balloon payment feature is popular when interest rates are high and/or when the buyer cannot otherwise qualify for a loan through a normal lender. If the three-year period arrives and you cannot get permanent financing, the balloon bursts and you lose the property and your large down payment.

4. You purchase a home on a land sales contract from an 85-year-old gentleman. The term of the contract is 15 years.

Strategy: It would be very prudent of you to insist that the owner execute a deed to you and put it in a neutral escrow to be delivered to you automatically when the debt is paid off. The same advice would pertain if the owner were in his twenties.

5. A homeowner who owns her home free and clear wants to finance it herself but won't accept an offer subject to a formal property inspection.

Strategy: There are times when owners avoid going through normal financing channels because they know there are problems with the property that an inspection or an appraisal would reveal. You have too much money riding on the transaction to gamble. Insist upon the inspection.

6. In negotiating a home purchase directly with the owner, you are told by him that a title insurance policy won't be needed since he just got one when he purchased the home a year ago.

Strategy: Title insurance policies insure what has occurred *before* the effective date, not what happens after. A new title search to uncover liens and other encumbrances must be done each time the property changes hands.

7. You are informed by a lending institution that the ARM loan they offer has a cap that will prevent your monthly payment from ever exceeding a certain specified amount.

Strategy: A payment cap on an ARM can result in negative amortization, since your payment may not cover all the interest due. Caps on the amount the rate can go up each year or for the life of the loan are preferable to other types of caps.

8. One lending institution features mortgages with a biweekly payment plan.

Strategy: If you pay your mortgage loan every other week, you will actually pay an extra month each year, since there are 52 weeks in a year. That means you will pay less interest over the life of the loan. It also means that you will constantly be writing checks. Why not take the 30-year loan with no prepayment penalty and pay any additional amount you want as frequently as you want?

9. A new home builder offers to buy down your mortgage loan to make it easier for you to qualify for a loan.

Strategy: Home builders (and other sellers, for that matter) will sometimes pay a fee to a lending institution to reduce a purchaser's interest rate for a year or two, which is called a buydown. That's a good deal, but remember that it is temporary and your interest rate and payments will go up after the expiration of the buydown. Permanent buydowns are rare.

10. Your REALTOR® tells you she knows of a lender who is offering a great deal on a discounted ARM.

Strategy: That's another name for a teaser rate. It is a temporary discount designed to induce you to take the loan. They are usually a percent or two below the actual going rate. They'll go up at the adjustment period.

15

▼

Judgment Day

It's the red-letter day you've been anticipating. In some areas of the country it's known as settlement. In other regions it's called close of escrow. Procedural details will also vary greatly, depending upon where you live. In some locations attorneys handle settlement, while in others escrow companies are used. Even real estate brokers and lenders frequently get into the act. You may attend the event with the sellers and all sit around a table and pass papers, or you may attend alone, depending on local custom. There are even a few places where much of this procedure is done by mail.

We will simply refer to the whole process as *closing*, but no matter what it's called or how it's done, the end result is the same. You will gleefully accept the deed and the keys to your newly purchased home and somewhat less gleefully hand over the remainder of the cash needed to officially wrap up the transaction. Since closing is also sometimes called the point of no return, it is important for you to know what will happen and how to ensure that your interests are best served.

It Ain't Easy Being a Homebuyer

If you've stayed with me to this point, I am certain you will agree that there is a great deal to know about buying a house. It's at closing that the entire process gets reduced to a handful of documents requiring your signature to seal the deal. There will be obscure legalistic language, a lot of very big numbers with dollar signs in front of them and you may get the feeling that everyone else involved seems to know a great deal more about what's going on than you do. But you will be very well prepared if you've paid attention and asked a lot of questions as you have proceeded. Let's recap certain events designed to help get you ready for your moment of truth.

Lender's Overview

When you first met informally with a lender for the prequalification interview, you were given an overview of typical costs associated with buying a home, a preview of different loan options and were qualified based on your assets, income and credit history. At that point you didn't have a specific home with a definite price tag in mind, so everything was simply an estimate. But the overview permitted you to establish a price range and an upper limit on what you would realistically be able to buy and get financed. You also got the sobering word on about how much cash you needed to amass to cover the down payment and other expenses.

Buyer's Net Sheet

You then selected a REALTOR® with whom to work, decided what agency relationship you were comfortable with, started looking at homes and made an offer on a home. At that point, although there is no federal law mandating it, the real estate agent should have prepared what is known as a buyer's net sheet for you. It would have contained a rough projection of what your cash outlay would be and what your monthly payments would run, assuming your offer were accepted and you got the financing you anticipated. When the offer was accepted, it should have been refined to reflect the actual price. An experienced REALTOR® can come very close to the true figures, since the agent will know what property taxes are running and will be very familiar with typical closing costs.

Lender's Good Faith Estimate

Even though you were prequalified for a loan, you still made your offer subject to both you and the property qualifying for financing. When you meet with a loan officer to formally submit an application, two things are required to happen, as provided for in the Real Estate Settlement Procedures Act (RESPA). First, the lender must give you a copy of a booklet called *Settlement Costs,* which is published by the U.S. Department of Housing and Urban Development (HUD). It's an informative little document that despite its small type, is worth reading very carefully. (Some lending institutions have printed their own upscale edition with larger print, but the information is the same.) Second, the lender must give you a good faith estimate of the settlement costs associated with your loan. If it isn't given to you on the day you apply (it almost always is), then it must be mailed to you within three days.

HUD Settlement Statement

One business day before close, you have the right to inspect the official HUD settlement form that must be used in almost all residential mortgage loans. It's the official tally sheet on who owes what to whom. There will be other items to sign at closing also, but this is the master document that's suppose to make everything clear. Even though your legal right is to be able to review the HUD settlement statement at least 24 hours in advance of closing, it is very wise if you can arrange to look at it before then. You will almost certainly have questions, and it's much better to get your answers when you don't have a pen in your hand ready to sign documents and when other people aren't looking at you impatiently.

Common Ground

All of these federally mandated requirements are designed to do one thing—protect homebuyers and homesellers. When investigations took place in the early 1970s, it was evident that there were widespread abuses in the settlement process and consumers were not well informed. The legislation doesn't mandate uniform settlement charges, so it does pay to shop around; and no matter how well you have educated yourself, it's still going to be a worthy challenge.

Closing Costs: The Gruesome Details

If you think sticker shock is a phenomenon restricted to new car buyers, you haven't bought a home lately. When you take a gander at the official closing statement, you may begin to wonder why you are paying for accessories you didn't think you ordered. Depending upon where you are located and the exact nature of the transaction, you may have to come up with as much as 3 to 6 percent of the sales price of the home in settlement costs at closing. That's in addition to your down payment. The key is to know ahead of time what you are going to have to pay and why.

The following is a rundown of some of the major costs you can encounter. We will cover them in the general order as they appear on the HUD settlement statement, and we'll use the same basic terminology.

Items Payable in Connection with the Loan

Although almost everything is negotiable as to who pays for what, you are borrowing the money, so you are usually required to pay the costs associated with getting the loan.

Loan Origination.   The official definition is that this is a fee to cover the lender's administrative costs. It is often expressed as a percentage of the loan. For example, if there is a 1 percent loan origination fee, that means a $1,000 charge on a $100,000 loan.

Loan Discount.   These are the infamous points. One point equals 1 percent of the mortgage amount. You pay points to increase the lender's yield on the money that they loan you. In many instances the loan origination fee and the points are lumped together into what are called fees and discount points. These costs can vary widely among lenders, so shopping around for the best deal is essential. Remember that the annual percentage rate (APR) lumps these costs into a more meaningful figure for you for comparative purposes.

Appraisal Fee.   The lender will insist upon a formal appraisal. The lender selects the appraiser and you pay for it. You should ask, in writing, for a copy of the appraisal report.

Credit Report Fee.   You may have paid for this fee up front. Otherwise, they catch it at the closing.

Lender's Inspection Fee.   If you are buying a newly constructed home, the bank will have it inspected at various stages.

Assumption Fee.   If you are assuming a loan that's already on the property, there will be an assumption fee.

Items Required by Lender To Be Paid in Advance

Interest.   This is one item that typically confuses borrowers. You are charged interest for the money you borrow from the day you get it until your normal payment schedule kicks in. For example, let's say you close on September 15 and your first payment is due November 1. Interest is paid in arrears, so your November payment covers October interest. You will pay for the September 15 to October 1 period at close.

Mortgage Insurance Premium.   Don't confuse this with mortgage life insurance or disability insurance. The mortgage insurance premium covers the lender in the event you default on your mortgage loan. Right—you pay. If you put less than 20 percent down, you will be required to have mortgage insurance. For a $100,000 loan, assuming a 10 percent down payment, the initial premium would be around $400, and there would be a monthly payment required of about $30.00. If you put 5 percent down, the mortgage insurance premium will be higher. As with many things in life, if you can afford a large up-front investment, it will save you money in the long run.

Hazard Insurance Premium.   The lender will obviously also insist that you insure your (and their) home against loss from fire, wind and other natural hazards. If you don't have formal evidence that you have already taken care of hazard insurance, the lender will require it before closing. Standard policies don't cover earthquake damage.

I strongly recommend you include it no matter where you live. If you live in a special flood hazard area, you may be required to carry flood insurance. Your lender will have details. If you are buying in an area with special perils, such as frequent wildfires and sinkholes, talk with the old-timer homeowners in the area for recommendations on appropriate coverage and an insurance company that doesn't become hard to locate when disaster strikes.

Reserves Deposited with Lenders

These may also be called impound accounts or escrow accounts. They are funds paid by you to the lender on a monthly basis to ensure that there is enough money to pay for such things as hazard insurance, mortgage insurance, property taxes and other assessments. If you put enough money down (20 percent minimum) on a conventional loan, you will probably be given the privilege of handling these things on your own. If the sellers have an impound account established, you will be required to reimburse them for the amount transferred to you at closing.

Title Charges

Title charges can vary widely, depending upon local practice and custom. Some of the standard fees to which you can look forward are as follows:

Settlement or Closing Fees. Whoever conducts the closing will charge a fee. It's often split between buyer and seller. The agreement to charge a settlement fee is frequently included in the standard offer-to-purchase forms.

Title Insurance. You want to know that the seller has good title and that if someone shows up later with a challenge, you will be insured against loss. In most areas the seller pays for what is known as the owner's title insurance policy. That seems reasonable to me, and I would insist upon title insurance even if you've been given a preliminary assessment by an attorney that title is good.

There also is a lender's title insurance policy that will be required, and—you guessed it—you will have to pay that fee. Title insurance is not terribly expensive, considered in the context of the other fees you will pay. A lender's policy, for example, might run a few dollars per thousand of the mortgage amount, which on a $100,000 loan would amount to a one-time charge of $200.

Government Recording and Transfer Charges

If you deal with reputable professionals, all appropriate documents, such as your new deed, will be recorded as a routine matter. You pay, but it's inexpensive. What isn't always inexpensive is any type of real property transfer tax that many states and localities have. Sellers are typically required to pay the most expensive of these charges, but it can have an impact on the entire transaction. It is important to know what the precise rules are where you plan to buy your home.

Buyer's Remorse

Buyer's remorse is a common malady. It can strike at just about any time after you have made an offer. Here's one possible scenario.

● ●

What Have I Done?

You've been so caught up in the whole homebuying adventure that you haven't really had time to think reflectively about what you are doing. The day before closing you receive your official settlement statement to review, and although you have a few questions, you get satisfactory answers to them and everything seems on course. The next morning you arise, look sleepily into the mirror and it suddenly hits you. "My God," you scream hysterically, "what have I done?" You just realized that you are about to walk out the door with a certified check for more money than you ever thought you would get together at one time and are about to commit to 30 years of house payments you aren't really sure you can afford on a home that is half as big and costs four times as much as the one in which you grew up. Your mate arrives with a pot of hot coffee and you eventually regain your composure, but that sick feeling in your stomach won't go away.

● ●

How To Avoid Buyer's Remorse

Even the most experienced, self-confident homebuyer is subject to at least a mild attack of buyer's remorse. Real estate agents are so accustomed to getting frantic late-night or early-morning calls from buyers who have become unglued that some have developed clever little techniques to deal with it. One particularly cutesy maneuver is to give buyers who have just received official notification that their offer has been accepted a small bottle filled with M&Ms along with instructions to "take two and call your real estate agent at the first symptom of buyer's remorse."

The best preventive measure is to be a knowledgeable, active participant in the entire process. It is critical that if you have questions, you get them answered to your satisfaction. If you don't completely understand a particular procedure or are not comfortable with an explanation you are given to a potential problem you spot, don't proceed until you are no longer ill at ease. It's also important to surround yourself with professionals whom you trust and upon whom you can rely.

Red Flag Checklist and Survival Strategies

1. When you are given your buyer's net sheet showing you what your closing and monthly costs will be on a home on which you are making an offer, it seems to be a lot less than you had anticipated.

Strategy: Real estate agents who are on the ball will prepare a very conservative buyer's net sheet to show a purchaser what to expect in the way of real dollar outlay. They don't want to underestimate, since that can erode confidence. Some less than forthright agents may intentionally give you lower figures to encourage you to go ahead and make the offer, with the assumption that if you really get caught up in the process you'll figure out a way to manage. Be informed and double-check the figures.

2. When you apply for your mortgage loan, you are told that it isn't covered by the Real Estate Settlement Procedures Act.

Strategy: Almost all residential loans are covered by RESPA, but there are a few exceptions. There is no reason the lender can't still give you a good faith estimate of fees and provide you with a copy of the HUD booklet *Settlement Costs*. You should also insist upon a closing statement with the information required by the standard HUD form.

3. *Your official settlement statement reflects a charge for a pest and dry-rot inspection, which the seller had agreed to pay.*

Strategy: Mistakes do occur. That's why it is important to go over the closing statement before you are actually required to officially sign off on it. The settlement statement should reflect prior written agreements between buyer and seller. You did get it in writing, didn't you?

4. *You ask your loan officer to explain what the document preparation charge is for on your good faith estimate. He responds, "It's a charge for preparing documents."*

Strategy: This is one of the several "gotcha" items you will have to pay. This charge is ostensibly for the preparation of documents such as mortgages, trust deeds and promissory notes, but those things are prepared as a matter of normal routine anyway without extra cost to the institution. It's really just an additional income generator for the lender. Remember the golden rule of lending.

5. *In preparing for closing, you are told that the lender will require a survey of the property, for which you will have to pay.*

Strategy: This may signal that the lender is concerned about encroachments from adjoining properties. If it is a large rural property, a survey could be expensive. Find out what motivates the requirement.

6. *A dispute arises just prior to the final settlement date over whether or not a particular piece of personal property was included in the sale.*

Strategy: The settlement process cannot proceed until both parties agree. No one can make a unilateral decision. That's why it's important to anticipate problems such as these ahead of time. If a dispute cannot be resolved, the whole process stops.

7. You conduct a final walk-through inspection of the house the day prior to settlement and notice that there are large shaded areas on the wall where pictures have been hung and that accumulated trash has not been removed from the garage.

Strategy: A final walk-through is critical, but it is better to schedule it several days before closing in the event that you find problems. The shaded areas are to be expected, but not the trash. Place a quick call to the real estate agent. Remember that no one gets paid until you sign off.

8. You are purchasing a home on a land sales contract and the closing is being handled by an escrow company. The seller informs you that his attorney will write up the contract so there will be no need for you to go to the expense of hiring an attorney.

Strategy: As a minimum, you would want your attorney to review the contract. Land sales contracts can be very flexible and must be tailored to fit the needs of the participants. Never rely on the advice of someone who represents the other party.

9. You get a call from the closing agent, who indicates that your instructions on how you wanted to take title to the property were not clear and that she needs an answer immediately if the transaction is to close on time.

Strategy: This is something you should have decided early as a matter of first priority and should have indicated when you made your offer to purchase. In any event you need legal counsel, since the rules vary so much from state to state. If you are buying with an unrelated person, there are special considerations. Some states have standard rules for husband and wife buyers that may not be appropriate for your situation. A quick phone call to your attorney should clear the matter up.

10. You ask your loan officer if you can have a copy of the appraisal that was done in connection with your loan. The response is, "It's not our policy to make those available since they are for bank purposes only."

Strategy: Ask for a copy of the appraisal in writing; they are required to give it to you. There will probably be disclaimers on the appraisal indicating that it is for the lender's use only; however, you paid for it, so you are entitled to it.

16

•••••▼•••••

And They Lived
Happily Ever After

There are several excellent reasons why you must do everything within your power to take the best possible care of your newly purchased home. First, if properly nurtured, your home can easily turn out to be the cornerstone of your vast financial empire. If you neglect and abuse your home, on the other hand, it may develop into a voracious alligator that you can't peddle to anyone else. Second, if you don't maintain your home in a manner your investment partners at the lending institution believe is appropriate, you may get some correspondence from them in very legalistic language that roughly translated will mean "shape up or ship out." Here are a few final thoughts on how to take maximum advantage of the American Dream.

Your Home As an Investment

You already know that I believe the major advantage of owning a home is that in most cases it will provide you with a lifestyle that is superior to other alternatives. You also know that I think it can be a great financial investment. How good? Ask many homeowners and they will say, "It's absolutely the best investment I ever made!" (Some may say it's the *only* good investment they ever made.)

My own personal experience may account for my unbridled enthusiasm. In my career in the air force we made several moves. With each move we bought a modest home in a nice neighborhood, took very good care of it and sold it for a handsome profit when we moved in three or four years. That was an incredibly shrewd plan of action on my part, right? Okay, I will give the air force partial credit for telling me to either move or get court martialed, but the basic principle is the same. Buy the right house, maintain and improve it and presuming the bottom doesn't fall out of your local housing market at the precise moment you must move and sell, you've bought a blue chip investment that Wall Street couldn't possibly match, inasmuch as you also get to live in it.

Appreciating Appreciation

You will often hear the term *leverage* used in connection with real estate investment. That simply means that when you buy a property, you use a lot of OPM (other people's money) and not much of your own.

From an investment standpoint, there's a balance you must strike when you are considering how much to leverage your investment in your home, assuming you have the flexibility to put more down than the very minimum to qualify for a loan. First, the obvious: The less money you put down, the more money you will have to borrow, the higher the interest rate and the larger your monthly payments. Second, it will also mean that you will probably incur other costs you would not have otherwise. For example, as we discussed earlier, if you put less than 20 percent down, you will have to pay a mortgage insurance premium at closing and each month until the balance of the loan is less than 80 percent of the value of the property. As we also pointed out, it will mean you will almost certainly have to establish a collection escrow for property taxes and insurance with the lender, which will mean a large chunk of money at closing and a monthly deposit that will be collected as part of your mortgage payment.

If you've scrapped and schemed to come up with the very minimum amount of cash required to qualify for a loan, then this whole discussion is academic. You can still profit from appreciation, and your eventual return on your initial investment could turn out to be spectacular. It's just that you will have to be a little more creative in meeting your other living expenses (such as eating) while making your monthly mortgage payment.

Taking Care of Business

At some point in the future it is quite likely that either you, or your heirs, will be selling your house. On the average, homeowners change residences every five years or so. That's why you should look at your home through the eyes of a potential buyer. There are several very practical things you can do to enhance your investment.

The "Good Neighbor" Policy.   You are fully aware by now that I am thoroughly convinced that real estate value is positively and dramatically influenced by the general appearance of a neighborhood; but if you're still a little skeptical, try this. Take a drive around your hometown. I'll wager you will find at least one locale where otherwise modest homes sell for a premium simply because the neighborhood is so neat and well kept. That being the case, let me suggest that there are two activities where your interests will be well served by doing a little neighborhood organizing: (1) appearance and (2) security.

1. *Fighting Grime.* Perhaps all of your new neighbors are *Better Homes and Gardens* freaks and keep their houses and grounds in immaculate condition. If that's the happy state of affairs, your challenge will be to hustle to keep pace and earn their admiring looks of approval as they stroll by your property. If that's not the case and some of the local denizens need a little encouragement to shake the lethargy and tidy things up, you would be surprised what a positive influence you can be by starting an upgrade project of your own.

   Begin with your front yard—that's where the words *curb appeal* originated. If you've bought a place that has a small Brazilian rain forest obscuring it, start by thinning and cutting. If you've got a fence that is rotting and leaning in six different directions, try to get enough money together to replace it. Do your best to get your immediate next-door neighbors involved, perhaps with a joint project on common border plantings or some help with that grungy fence. My experience is that these activities often become contagious and that others will soon start trying to emulate their energetic neighbors. I guarantee it will happen if folks make the cause-and-effect relationship between the enhanced appearance and market value. A good sale or two will do that.

2. *Fighting Crime.* There are times when it pays to be a little nosey. If a large van is backed up to your neighbor's house and is loading up its entire contents, it would be good for you to know whether or not they are being ripped off or are actually moving (by choice). It all starts by knowing who your neighbors are and having a roster of names and telephone numbers. Periodic neighborhood watch meetings in which security measures are discussed are extremely valuable. In most cities local law enforcement authorities will gladly send a crime prevention representative. It is very reassuring to prospective purchasers to know that a neighborhood is security conscious and that people are concerned about looking out after each other's welfare.

Maintenance.   Routine maintenance is essential so that minor problems don't turn into major ones. As a result of the inspections, both personal and professional, you should be well informed as to potential problem areas. If your state has a property disclosure law, you were also given a detailed checklist on the home you bought. If there is no such requirement where you reside, get a copy of one from some other source. (California's property disclosure law is a good one. See Chapter 12.) You can use the checklist as a handy guide for your maintenance efforts. You don't want any major surprises when it's time to sell and you must fill out a property disclosure form.

Improvements.   Even if you move into a brand-new home, you may soon discover that you and/or your mate would love to add a little here and/or demolish a little there. My first suggestion is to evaluate very carefully before you decide upon a home improvement project. Be absolutely certain that you are really improving your house and that a potential purchaser will view it in the same manner. I once listed a home where the expansive and luxurious master bedroom and bath were redone exclusively in pink. Padded pink wallpaper. Pink tile. Pink countertops. Everything was pink—shocking pink. We eventually found buyers who liked the home, but they discounted their offer substantially to take into account what it was going to cost them for a major makeover. Construction experts seem to agree that kitchen and bathroom remodeling give you the biggest payoff when you sell.

My second piece of advice is not to wait until your house is falling apart to start remodeling. If you can figure out a way to finance smaller individual projects as you progress, you won't be faced with the mega-costs and intense trauma of a major remodeling project. As I write this, our frumpy old homestead is undergoing massive reconstructive surgery. Two of the three baths are scarred, empty shells awaiting their upscale new fixtures. The old kitchen is completely gone, and I'm pretty sure the gaping hole in the wall is going to be the new see-through feature to the dining room that my wife seems so thrilled with. On this very day the painter, plumber, electrician and contractor are scheduled to arrive. The electrician spends a lot of his time looking over my shoulder at the computer screen as I write and offers constructive criticism on what I should be telling you, and the temperamental painter keeps asking how he is supposed to work in such a madhouse. Our dog has developed a serious whining problem, and our cat has retreated to the back of his house and won't come out. We are all so tired of frozen dinners from the microwave that we could scream (and frequently do—at each other). If we had it to do over, we might not. At least we wouldn't have waited until bulldozing the whole place was a viable alternative. Some who have gone through this process suggest that the wedding vows be changed to "until death or a major remodeling do us part."

Dealing with Count Taxula.   If you look several years into the future, here is what you might see. Your little bungalow has almost doubled in value, and you have decided to sell, rent an apartment and enjoy the fruits of your windfall profit. The shock that you get when your accountant tells you what the taxes will be on your gain may cause you to reconsider your plans.

If you sell and then rent, you will pay income tax on the difference between what you paid for your home (plus improvements you made to it) and what you sold it for (less the costs of selling it). You could be looking at very big bucks in the way of profit, and you may be faced with paying almost half of it in federal and state taxes, depending upon where you live. Thus, there are a few alternatives you should consider.

The first alternative is that if you buy or build another primary residence of equal or greater value within a two-year period, you can defer paying taxes on your gain. Note that I said *defer*, not *forgive*. Check with your accountant for the latest specifics since the details may change, but I'm guessing the basic benefit will remain intact for the foreseeable future. Too many voters would be outraged if they changed the law much.

The second alternative is that if you hold on until you are age 55 or over, you can claim a one-time exemption on any capital gains profit up to $125,000 from selling your primary residence. Things can get a little tricky if there are situations such as a former spouse, so make certain you have good counsel. At some point in the future, if the senior citizen lobby is strong enough, this benefit may be tied to an escalation feature to take into account inflation, but such is not the case now.

Blue Plate Special: Buy-and-Hold Strategy

You will recall that in Chapter 7 we discussed the case of Dr. Sam, who bought a duplex as his first home, lived in one side and rented out the other, and later kept the duplex as an investment when he had his dream house built. That suggests a strategy you may wish to consider.

Most people only sell their home and move when the situation demands. How about this? Every four or five years why not buy a new home but keep the old one as a rental? After 15 or 20 years you would have several houses that should provide a very positive cash flow for you and a substantial boost to your net worth. You see, when you originally buy each property, you will qualify for an owner-occupant loan, which is the best mortgage rate offered. But no law says you have to remain an owner-occupant forever.

You will recognize immediately that this is a plan not entirely without drawbacks and potential hazards. First, not everyone wants to move every few years, no matter what the payoff is. Second, even if that isn't a problem, it may be tough to afford a new home without selling the old one, although refinancing and pulling out equity money is also a possibility. Third, rents have to provide a positive cash flow, but inflation normally handles that nicely.

Here's another possibility. When you sell a home that has appreciated in value, there's an excellent chance that you will have more cash than you need to put down on a new primary residence. That's how we were able to afford the condo in which my wife's mother lived for several years. You will pay a little higher interest rate for non-owner-occupied property, but money is usually available. When we first started renting the condo, we got $375 per month, which resulted in a very slight aftertax negative cash flow. Ten years later the rent is $775 and the assessed value has increased over 400 percent. Our only regret is that we didn't try to figure out a way to buy a few other rental properties.

I must point out that to pursue these options, you must be temperamentally suited to being a landlord. Not all of us are. My wife is; I am not. Very few of us are prepared for the rigors of being an absentee landlord, so let me make sure you understand that I'm talking about homes you can drive by occasionally to ensure that they are still in the same basic configuration as they were when you rented them out.

If you decide to become a landlord on even a modest basis, you need to do some serious studying on your own and enlist the efforts of a competent accountant to get you headed in the right direction. I've included a few reference books in the Bibliography that will prove helpful, and there almost always are property management organizations locally that you can join to share ideas with others with common interests.

Happy Homebuying!

Touting the virtues of home ownership to those of you who are or have been homeowners may be like preaching to the choir. You may already be dedicated converts. For you it's just a matter of becoming fully informed on current laws and market conditions, getting started and staying alert. However, if this is your first time around, you may occasionally stop, survey the whole complicated situation and ask yourself, "Is this really worth all the effort?" Of course nothing is certain except for you know what and you know what, but for generations home ownership has truly been the American Dream come true. It can be for you. Happy homebuying!

Bibliography

•••••▼•••••

Homebuying Reference Books

Allen, Robert. *Nothing Down for the 90's.* New York: Simon and Schuster, 1990. Buying a home for nothing down is not impossible—just highly improbable. Despite that reservation, reading Allen's book will prove to be very instructive. Just keep your feet on the ground.

Boroson, Warren, and Ken Austin. *The Home Buyer's Inspection Guide.* New York: John Wiley & Sons, 1993. There are a lot of excellent home inspection books on the market. This is one of the best I've seen. It is well illustrated and won't scare you off with a lot of incomprehensible technical terms.

Bull, Diana, and Elaine St. James. *The Equity Sharing Book.* New York: Penguin Books, 1990. A lot of equity sharing goes on in California, the home of these two practicing REALTORS®. If the topic interests you, this is a good place to start.

Cooper, Cynthia. *Homeowner's Legal Guide.* Yonkers, N.Y.: Consumer Reports Books, 1993. While this guide will be of primary value to you after you become a homeowner, it's an excellent basic reference.

Edwards, Kenneth. *Your Successful Real Estate Career.* New York: American Management Association, 1993. If you become so fascinated by the entire homebuying enterprise that you finally decide to fulfill your sainted mother's dream to have a licensed real estate agent in the family, this is the book to read. It is authoritative and witty. The fact that I wrote it has nothing to do with my glowing endorsement.

Fields, Alan, and Denise Fields. *Your New House*. Boulder, Colo. Windsor Peak Press, 1993. If you are thinking about buying or building a new home, you really owe it to yourself to read this book first (unless you are the type who discourages easily). It is entertaining as well as informative. You think I'm tough on real estate agents? Alan and Denise Fields counsel you to "treat your real estate agent like a dog" (scold, praise, treats, etc.). Now that's tough.

Harrison, Henry. *Houses*. 2d ed. Chicago: Dearborn Financial Publishing, 1992. The subtitle to this book is "The Illustrated Guide to Construction, Design & Systems." The book contains everything you will need to know about those subjects. It's an excellent basic reference.

Hoven, Vernon. *Real Estate Investor's Tax Guide*. Chicago: Dearborn Financial Publishing, 1993. This guide will tell you a lot more than you need to know about taxes as a homeowner. But if you decide you want to get a little fancy with other real estate investments, this is a great reference.

Irwin, Robert. *Tips & Traps When Buying a Home*. New York: McGraw-Hill, 1990. The format of this book is intriguing because it does in fact offer the homebuyer many excellent tips for avoiding traps.

Kiplinger. *Buying & Selling a Home*. 4th ed. Washington, D.C.: Kiplinger Books, 1993. If you have only one homebuying book (other than the one you are reading, of course), make it this one. This is the fourth edition of a book that the staff of *Kiplinger's Personal Finance Magazine* produces. It has an incredible amount of excellent resource material and is written in a style that's reader friendly. When you hear of exotic new homebuying fantasies, come back to this book for a reality check.

Kollen, Melissa. *Buying Real Estate Foreclosures*. New York: McGraw-Hill, 1992. Kollen got her start by locating and purchasing foreclosure properties for an investment group in New York. Her book provides excellent guidance on how to work with professionals who are experienced in foreclosure matters.

Lank, Edith. *The Homebuyer's Kit*. 2d ed. Chicago: Dearborn Financial Publishing, 1991. Lank writes the syndicated question-and-answer real estate column "House Calls." This book is clear, concise and authoritative.

Lank, Edith, and Miriam Geisman. *Your Home as a Tax Shelter*. Chicago: Dearborn Financial Publishing, 1993. This book will tell you what you need to know about the tax advantages of home ownership without glazing your eyeballs in the process.

Miller, Peter. *The Common Sense Mortgage: 1993 Edition*. New York: Harper & Row, Publishers, 1993. Miller has hit upon the dream project of all authors—a book so popular he revises it almost every year. If you feel compelled to learn more about real estate finance, this is the book to read. Miller writes in a very relaxed, yet authoritative, style. You'll find it easy to follow.

Reed, John. *Residential Property Acquisition Handbook*. Danville, Calif.: Reed Publishing, 1993. Reed is a veteran no-nonsense real estate investor and a prolific author. While this particular book is aimed primarily at investors, it provides comprehensive basic information for homebuyers. It is available from Reed Publishing, 342 Bryan Drive, Danville, CA 94526. Ask for a catalog of publications.

Reilly, John. *The Language of Real Estate*. Chicago: Dearborn Financial Publishing, 1993. If you want a good basic real estate reference, this is the best "you could look it up" book on the market. It's part dictionary and part encyclopedia. Reilly is an attorney with a lively sense of communication. From "AAA tenant" to "zoning estoppel," you'll find entries that tell you what you need to know without overwhelming you.

Robinson, Leigh. *Landlording*. 6th ed. El Cerrito, Calif.: ExPress, 1992. If you follow my buy-and-hold real estate investment strategy, you will want to have a copy of this book handy at all times. If you insist that a book must be dull to be authoritative, look elsewhere. Robinson is an active property manager who updates this book frequently. It's privately published but available at bookstores.

Sher, Carol, and Les Sher. *Finding & Buying Your Place in the Country*. Chicago: Dearborn Financial Publishing, 1992. This book is an exhaustive treatment of the subject. It has become the standard national reference on buying country homes. It is practical and, appropriately, down-to-earth.

Ventura, John. *The Credit Repair Kit*. Chicago: Dearborn Financial Publishing, 1993. If you have credit problems, this is a good source document for you. Check this book out before you spend money to consult with a credit counselor.

Vila, Bob. *Bob Vila's Guide to Buying Your Dream House*. New York: Little, Brown & Co., 1990. This is an exceptionally well-researched book. It's particularly strong in the area of recognizing a structurally sound home, reflecting Vila's "This Old House" expertise.

Wiedemer, James. *The Homeowner's Guide to Foreclosure*. Chicago: Dearborn Financial Publishing, 1993. Wiedemer is an experienced foreclosure lawyer. This book offers guidance on how to avoid foreclosure, but it's an excellent basic resource for the homebuyer as well.

Index